A CULTURAL-INSIGHT GUIDE

Why Mexicans Think & Behave the Way They Do!

The Cultural Factors that Created
the Character & Personality
of the Mexican People!

Boyé Lafayette De Mente

A Phoenix BOOKS ORIGINAL

Phoenix Books/Publishers
ISBN: 0-914778-56-0

OTHER BOOKS BY THE AUTHOR

Japanese Etiquette & Ethics in Business
I Like You, Gringo—But! (With Mario
"Mike" De La Fuente)
Korean Etiquette & Ethics in Business
Korean in Plain English
Japanese in Plain English
Chinese Etiquette & Ethics in Business
Businessman's Quick-Guide to Japan
The Grand Canyon Answer Book
Survival Japanese
Japan Made Easy—All You Need to Know to Enjoy
Japan
Diner's Guide to Japan
Shopper's Guide to Japan
Etiquette Guide to Japan
Instant Japanese
Japan's Cultural Code Words
Chinese in Plain English
China's Cultural Code Words
Mexican Cultural Code Words
Korea's Business & Cultural Code Words
Korean Business Etiquette
There is a Word for it in Mexico
KATA—The Key to Understanding & Dealing With
the Japanese
Asian Face Reading—Unlock the Secrets Hidden
in the Human Face
The Japanese Samurai Code—Classic Strategies for
Success

Samurai Strategies—42 Martial Secrets from
Musashi's Book of Five Rings (The Samurai Way of
Winning)
Cultural Code Words of the Navajo People
Cultural Code Words of the Hopi People
Instant Chinese
Survival Chinese
Instant Korean
Survival Korean
Mistress-Keeping in Japan—The Pitfalls & the
Pleasures
Etiquette Guide to Korea
Etiquette Guide to China
THE CHINESE MIND – Understanding Traditional
Chinese Beliefs and Their Influence on
Contemporary Culture
Why the Japanese Are a Superior People!—The
Advantages of Using Both Sides of Your Brain!
The Myth of Intelligent Life on Planet Earth!

ACKNOWLEDGEMENTS

I am deeply grateful to the following people for critiquing the manuscript of this book, and sharing with me their knowledge of Mexico and the Mexican way of doing business:

Jack Scott
Founder and Chairman of the Board
of Key International
Scottsdale, Arizona

Ronald C. Walker*
Business Consultant/Mexico

Dirk A. Weisheit*
Marketing Specialist / Consultant – Mexico

Michael T. Eakins*
Marketing Specialist – Mexico

Walter J. Gomez*
Marketing Specialist – Mexico

Alberto A. Medina
Marketing Specialist / Consultant – Mexico

Lorenzo De La Fuente M.
Businessman & Entrepreneur, Nogales, Mexico

*Ronald C. Walker, Dirk A. Weisheit, Michael T. Eakins and Walter J. Gomez hold Master of International Management degrees from Thunderbird School of Global Management, where they specialized in Latin American studies.

Contents

Introduction

Behind the Masks of Mexico

(1)
Survival of the Fittest

(2)
Intellectual & Spiritual Mexico

(3)
The Mexican Character Today

Cultural Regions of Mexico
Personalismo / Coping with a Hostile World
Moralidad / Dealing with Situational Ethics
Dignidad / The Importance of Dignity and Face
Respeto / The Toreador Syndrome
Cortesia / Living in Virtual Reality
Critica / Taboos Against Criticism
Responsabilidad / Avoiding Responsibility
La Verdad / Mexican-Style Truth
Imagen / The Mexican Self-Image
Lealtad / The Human Equation
Simpatico / The Sympathy Syndrome
Buena Gente / One of the Good Guys
Machismo / The Masculinity Cult
Mucha Mujer / The Femininity Cult
Santas / Women as Saints
Serpientes / Women as Serpents
Emancipacion / More Freedom for Women
Mujeres y Negocios / Women and Business
Hora Mexicana / Dealing with Polychronic People
Paciencia / The Virtue of Patience
El Nacionalismo / Pride and Prejudice
Extranjeros / The Gringo Syndrome
Hospitalidad / Making Friends and Influencing People
Espanol / To Speak or Not to Speak
Obscenidades y Vulgaridades / Obscenities and
Vulgarities
La Realimentacion / Feedback Mexican Style
Realidad / Dealing With Mexican Reality
Fatalismo / Life Without Hope

INTRODUCTION

BEHIND THE MASKS OF MEXICO

Mexicans are acutely aware that their country is unique, and there is a popular saying to that effect: *Como Mexico no hay dos!* (Coh-moh MEH-he-coh no aye dohss!)—There is no other country like Mexico!"

This saying is true in a geographical and racial sense as well as in a broad spectrum of cultural and ethnic differences. The majority of Mexicans—some 80 percent—are *Mestizos* (Mes-TEE-zohs), a "new race" made up of a Spanish-Indian blend. Their character is also a merger, made up of traditional Indian and Spanish authoritarianism, medieval Catholicism, personalism, machoism, and, despite the negative aspects of these influences, an inherently joyful nature that manifests itself in music, singing, dancing and art.

Because of historical circumstances, Mexico's traditional ethics were forged in a caldron of aggressive religious intolerance, corruption, racism, male chauvinism, and an elitist political system that connived to keep ordinary people ignorant and powerless and to deny them the most basic human rights.

From the beginning of the Spanish colonial period in Mexico in 1521 the Indians who survived the conquest and the Mestizo descendants of the conquistadors (who were to eventually become the majority) were systematically victimized by an authoritarian and venal government and an equally self-centered Catholic Church.

In this setting, the day-to-day ethics of virtually all Mexicans—Spanish, Mestizos and Indians alike—were reduced to the personal level and were based on the circumstances at hand rather than universal principles of right and wrong. Generally, people who were in positions of civil and ecclesiastical auth-ority used their power to benefit themselves, their families and their friends at the expense of everyone else. Those without power lived and died according to circumstances over which they had little or no control.

Another characteristic of Mexico's traditional culture was that both the nature and the defining role of Mexican ethics were masked behind a public facade of highly stylized and courtly etiquette that was impressive to outsiders but gave a false image of the realities of Mexican life. In fact, the reality of Mexico has traditionally been obscured behind masks of piety, pride, courage, gaiety, indifference and stoicism.

Masks—the real kind—have long been of extraordinary importance in Mexico. They were traditionally used by Mexican Indians and Indianized Mestizos to communicate with the spirit world, to act out the roles of gods, goddesses and spirits, to create imaginary worlds, and to signify mystery, power, and sometimes ruthlessness.

On a more mundane level, Mexicans also have a long tradition of assuming mask-like facial expressions as a protective cloak to conceal their thoughts from outsiders in order to avoid loss of face or getting involved in situations that could be physically dangerous or threaten their position in society.

The various uses of masks and masked expressions by Mexicans have their exact counterparts among the people of the Orient. In fact, Mexico's traditional ethics and etiquette are more Oriental than Western in that they often do not follow the patterns of linear thought that are characteristic of the Anglo-Western mindset. Because of the personal and generally emotional foundation of Mexican attitudes and behavior, Mexicans have traditionally been more difficult for Anglo Westerners to understand, accept, and deal with effectively.

Despite the dramatic economic, political and social changes that have been taking place in Mexico since the last decades of the 20th century, the attitudes and behavior of most Mexicans remain very traditional in all of their personal and business relationships. It is therefore important that people dealing with Mexico be familiar with the nature of Mexico's traditional morality, ethics and etiquette, and develop skill in transcending the differences they encounter.

Veteran expatriate businesspeople in Mexico almost always distill the advice they give to newcomers down to six words: *Study the history of the country!*

Boyé Lafayette De Mente

(1)
SURVIVAL
OF THE FITTEST

Mexico before Columbus

Mexico has been inhabited for at least 30,000 years, and long before the appearance of any of the modern people of Europe had given birth to several great civilizations. [Archaeologists say that some 10,000 sites of ancient cities have been identified in central Mexico alone.]

The greatest of these civilizations included the Olmecs, Teotihuacanos, Toltecs, Mayans, Zapotecs and Mexicas (commonly called Aztecs*), whose economic, social and scientific achievements paralleled—and in some instances predated—those of early African, Asian and European civilizations. But also like most of their Asian and European counterparts, the earliest Mexican civilizations rose, flowered for a number of centuries then fell, often leaving nothing behind but myths and artifacts made of stone and metal.

---

*"'Aztec' was the Spanish term applied to this civilization, whereas most Mexican historians consider 'Mexica' (MEH-he-cah) to be more accurate"—Ronald C. Walker, Consultant/Mexico.

The last of these great Mexican civilizations, the Mexicas (or Aztecs as they are better known), who were the dominant civilization in central Mexico at the time of the Spanish arrival, survived for less than 100 years after achieving supremacy in 1428 A.D. The Aztecs, along with the other Indians of pre-Columbian Mexico, lived under governments and religions that exercised absolute power and controlled virtually every aspect of their lives. A number of Mexico's Indian nations practiced human sacrifice as a key part of their religious rituals, maintained slaves, and imposed the death penalty for what is now regarded as relatively minor offenses, ensuring a very orderly society.

Despite these fundamental differences from contemporary societies, Mexico's Indians were skilled artists and craftsmen, reveled in competitive and spectator sports, and had long traditions of music, singing, dancing and poetry. The ruling and upper classes lived in ostentatious luxury. Their great cities were as impressive as any in the world at that time.

As had often been the case historically, it was to be the arrival of a new people on the scene that brought the Aztecs and all other Mexican Indians down. But this time it was to be a totally alien people from another world that would change Mexico forever.

Clash of Conquerors

Only 31 years after Columbus stumbled upon the islands of the Caribbean in 1492, Spanish *conquistadores* (cone-kees-tah-DOHR-ehs) or "conquerors" were the masters of Mexico, which, at that time, had a population that some historians estimate as high as 21 to 25 million, made up of over 100 native tribal nations. [The population of Spain in the 15th century was around eight million.]

The policy of the Spanish conquerors was simple: slaughter the Indians who resisted them, convert those who surrendered to colonialism and Catholicism, and turn them into slaves or workers indentured for life.

The *conquistadores* were a driven people, obsessed with a lust for riches and glory, for themselves, for Spain and for the Catholic Church. They were equally obsessed with the righteousness of their cause, and saw no evil in the death and destruction they inflicted upon the Aztecs and other inhabitants of Mexico.

But the Aztecs were also a formidable people, equal if not superior to the Spaniards in their will to power, their courage and skill at arms, and in their brutal treatment of enemies.

The Spaniards won Mexico because of a series of remarkable coincidences and circumstances that had nothing to do with their own abilities or goals.

Moctezuma, the mythic-minded Aztec emperor, believed that Hernan Cortes was the legendary Toltec king Quetzalcoatl who had returned to lay rightful claim to his throne, and literally handed the great city of Tenochtitlan [Mexico City*] and himself over to the Spaniards.

---

*Mexicans seldom say "Mexico City." They generally call the capital "Mexico D.F." in formal references, and simply "Mexico" on other occasions—as in "I'm going to Mexico."

Within less than a year, one of Cortes' lieutenants had used the occasion of a festival to slaughter several hundred unarmed members of Moctezuma's Court including most of his top military commanders and leading priests. Cortes had also greatly increased the number of Spanish troops under his command; smallpox brought into the Aztec capital by the Spaniards had killed several thousand high-level Aztecans, and thousands more were to die from the unknown disease.

Finally aroused to action, the surviving Aztec leaders rallied their troops against Cortes and his men and nearly annihilated them when they tried to sneak out of the capital at night. Cortes was one of the Spaniards who survived the battle. Within a few months he had organized a new army of Spanish *conquitadores* and conspired with several Indian nations to lay a naval blockade around the lake-bound city of Tenochtitlan to starve its inhabitants and defenders into submission.

Cortes' strategy, combined with the ravages of small-pox which had continued sweeping through the Aztec capital like a plague, worked. Tenochtitlan, one of the largest and most magnificent cities in the world at that time, was sacked then destroyed.

For the next several decades, Cortes' successors continued the campaign against the Mexican nations that chose to fight rather than surrender, eventually subjugating or destroying all except a few in the more remote regions of the country.

Over the next several decades the Spanish rulers of Mexico, which they renamed New Spain, systematically destroyed the political, economic and religious foundations of what had been a flourishing way of life for the Indians of Mexico, turned the country into a colonial appendage of Spain, isolated it from the rest of the world, and inadvertently set the stage for the creation of a new race of people and a new nation that only now is coming into its own.

The Sexual Conquest of Mexico
One of the most extraordinary "policies" practiced by the Spanish conquerors of Mexico was miscegenation on a massive scale. Virtually from the first day of their landing on the Gulf coast of Mexico, Hernan Cortes and his men began having sexual intercourse with Indian girls and women at practically every opportunity. And it was not always the Spaniards who initiated sexual liaisons with Mexican Indians.

When Aztec emperor Moctezuma was informed by courier that a group of god-like white men had landed on the shores of Mexico he quickly sent 20 young women to them to serve as their personal slaves and sex partners—a custom the Spaniards had previously encountered in Cuba and other islands of the Caribbean, and had come to expect.

Cortes, the main figure in the conquest of Mexico, had in fact used the lure of women as well as gold, titles, and glory when recruiting men for his army.

But as a Catholic in good standing, he would not allow his men to have sexual intercourse with Indian women until they had been baptized, given Spanish names, and registered as Catholic converts—a process happily (for the Spaniards) took only a few minutes for the whole lot.

The Spanish obsession for having sex with Indian women was not just to satisfy an extraordinary lust or live up to a hyper macho image—and the latter was certainly an important factor. It was also done to impregnate as many Indian women as possible in order to create a new population of "non-Indians"—a practice that had evolved from earlier contacts with native populations in Cuba and elsewhere in the Caribbean, and had the tacit if not outright approval of the Catholic Church.

In fact, many of the Catholic priests who followed in the footsteps of Spain's *conquistadores* also took up the practice of miscegenation with equally extraordinary energy. During the second century of the Spanish colonial period there were numerous instances when priests exceeded the very liberal customs of the day and became so blatant in sexually serving their mostly female flock that they were frequently admonished by the Church.

Soon after the fall of the Aztec empire the Spanish Crown decreed that *conquistadores* who had been rewarded by being given grants of land had to marry within three years in order to have their titles to the land officially confirmed. The grants, called *encomiendas* (en-coh-me-ENdahs), included all of the Indians on the land. This resulted in a flurry of mar-riages between the Spanish conquerors and their Indian mistresses.

The mixed-blood offspring of these legal unions, called Mestizos, as well as the children sired by Cortes and his top lieutenants with their mistresses, were raised as "white" members of the Spanish community in Mexico.

But the practicing of raising Mestizos as whites and accepting them into Spanish society did not survive long after the passing of the original *conquistadores*.

Most Spanish administrators and military occu-pation forces in Mexico, married or not, continued to exercise sexual rights over Indian females in their employ or under their control, resulting in more and more mixed-bloods being born out of wedlock. As the decades passed, the mixed-bloods became a class of apart, not accepted by either the Spanish or Indian com-munities.

The fecundity and energy of the Spanish overlords of Mexico is starkly revealed in the population figures taken at intervals during the 300-year long Spanish reign (1521 to 1821).

Despite the fact that European diseases brought to Mexico by the Spaniards killed some 90 percent of the Indian population of the country within the first 100 years of the Spanish reign, the population of Mestizos continued to spiral upward—in later generations primarily from inter-marriages among themselves.

In 1650 church and municipal records show there were some 160,000 Mestizos in Mexico—with over 30,000 of this number in Mexico City, where they were regarded as *leperos* or "social lepers." Most of the Mestizos in the capital worked as manual laborers, but many lived primarily by scavenging and stealing.

By 1810, when Mexico began its war for inde-pendence from Spain, there were some 1.5 million

Mestizos in the country, one million pure Spanish-blooded residents born in Mexico, and some 80,000 residents who had been born in Spain and were assigned to the country as colonial administrators or had come to Mexico as immigrants from Spain and other Spanish colonies.

By this time, the Indian population, which had fallen as low as around one million in the early 1600s, had recovered to around 3.5 million.

In 1910, when the Mexican revolution began to oust dictator Porfirio Diaz and the military and Church complex that ruled the country, there were eight million Mestizos, 1,150,000 pure or nearly pure European Mexicans, and around 6 million Indians. It was during this period of revolutionary turmoil that the Mestizos of Mexico first became fully aware that they were in the majority, that they had become a new race of people, that they were *the Mexicans*, and that Mexico was—or should be—theirs.

When the revolution ended in 1917 (some historians say 1921 because the violence continued sporadically), the absolute monopoly that the Church and military had exercised over the country for 400 years had been broken.

But the 300-year Spanish regime and the following 100 years of authoritarian rule by home-grown dictators had left a cultural imprint on the minds and psyche of the Mexicans that still today is the foundation of Mexican ethics and etiquette.

Devils in Priests' Robes

During the 15th century, the Catholic Pope in Rome and his army of cardinals, bishops and priests ruled much of Europe in name as well as in fact. The Pope made and unmade kings and emperors, and those who sat on the thrones of Europe usually did so only with the blessing and support of the Pope. The Catholicism of that period (and for the next four centuries) was a predatory and intolerant religion that did not accept any other religious belief or practice, or take no for an answer.

Members of the Roman Catholic Church who did not accept all of the Church dogma were sought out with fanatical zeal and some were subjected to the most heinous torture. Those who did not recant their heresy were excommunicated and generally burned to death.

Non-white people who lived outside the sphere of Christianity, Judaism and Islam, especially people who still lived in tribal societies and societies with primitive or non-European cultures, were regarded by the Catholic Church as savage heathens who had no political or religious rights of their own.

The Catholic Church also presumed that it had a mandate from the Christian God to destroy the native religions and practices of heathens and to convert them to Christianity by persuasion if possible and by the sword if necessary. This was the religion that Hernan Cortes and his band of *conquistadores* brought to Mexico in 1519.

The missionary army of the Roman Catholic Church itself was only a few steps behind Cortes and his men, for the religious zeal of the Catholic Church equaled if not surpassed the lust of Spain's conquerors for gold and glory. Just a few days after Cortes and his men landed on the eastern coast of Mexico in 1519 they rescued a Catholic priest who had been with an earlier party of explorers that had been shipwrecked, and was living with an Indian tribe. He agreed to join Cortes' band of fortune hunters, thereby adding to the moral justification for the enterprise.

The first contingent of Franciscan priests arrived in Mexico from Spain less than two years after Cortes had destroyed the Aztec empire. They were quickly followed by groups of Dominicans and Augustinians, and later by Jesuits as well.

Immediately upon arriving in Mexico, the Catholic priests ordered the destruction of all Indian temples, religious artifacts, books and anything else that appeared to have a religious significance to the native people. (Veteran businessman and long-time student of Mexico Dirk Weisheit says: "The loss to history was incalculable!")

In the areas that were under their control, the priests also prohibited any kind of native Indian ceremony or festival, and began a massive program to wean the inhabitants away from their own languages and instruct them in the liturgy and dogma of Catholicism. The goal of the Catholic Church was to totally erase the native Indian cultures, their spiritual as well as their physical worlds, and replace them with Spanish-Catholic culture—a process that Mexican philosopher-writer Octavio Paz later said left the Indians of Mexico in a solitude so profound that it could not be imagined by anyone else.

To their credit, the goals of the first Catholic priests in Mexico were good-intentioned from their perspective. But good intentions were not enough to prevent the corruption that developed within the Church as the decades passed. By the end of the first century of Spanish rule in Mexico the quality of the priests had dropped so low that critics described the majority of them as having no faith and no morals.

The Mexican Church had become a money-making machine and used its growing wealth, derived from charging for its services and from gifts received from rich silver miners and others, to buy nearly 50 percent of all the real estate in Mexico. Historians say it had mortgages on much of the rest of the country. Most of the priests assigned to Mexico during the two additional centuries of the Spanish reign were obsessed with accumulating more wealth and power for the Church and themselves. The lust and venery of many of them was unbounded.

All attempts to educate the Indians in the Spanish and Catholic cultures had virtually ended by 1650, as nearly 90 percent of the entire Indian population had died from European diseases, mistreatment and culture shock, and the operators of the country's great silver mines, haciendas and plantations were more interested in mute, passive laborers and serfs than in educated employees.

During the entire span of the Spanish regime in Mexico the Catholic Church was in charge of all education, recording births, providing marriage licenses and death certificates, and conducting the various rites of passage that were an essential part of the lives of the people.

In its arrogant greed, the Church treated the surviving Indians and growing number of Mestizo outcasts with cruel disdain, deliberately keeping them ignorant and emotionally and spiritually dependent upon the Church.

This environment resulted in a majority of the poor men of Mexico developing a sublime but usually quiet and passive contempt for the Church. For women, however, the Church was their only refuge, and it controlled much of their lives.

Thus for more than 300 years the Church of Mexico was like a parasite, sucking away at the spirit and soul of the Indians and Mestizos, even more responsible for their poverty and powerlessness than the colonial government and its dictatorial successors because it controlled their minds.

"And yet," adds Ronald C. Walker, business consultant and specialist in Mexican history, "the Church provided the only refuge, beyond the family, in which the disenfranchised could seek succor and any kind of education."

Although a new breed of Catholic priest who is dedicated to the spiritual and physical welfare of the people has finally come to the fore in the Catholic Church of Mexico, most rural Mexicans are still in the throes of extracting themselves from the legacy of centuries of domination by the Church and the state.

Much of the evil that still exists in Mexican culture, from the various forms of institutionalized bribery to the failures of law enforcement and the justice system, can be traced to the immoralities and injustices condoned, and committed, by the Church for so many generations.

But, adds Ronald C. Walker: "Again it is important to keep in mind that in the context of 16th to 20th century world history, the beliefs and activities of the Catholic Church were probably not much different in Mexico than in Europe and other parts of the world.

"The intangible element of religious solace provided by Catholicism to the impoverished masses in a society where scant trust could be placed in government or neighbors is a difficult quality to quantify in the history of Mexico. But examples of religious-inspired fortitude are incredibly common in Mexican history—even today. A good case can also be made that Mexican patience—although viewed by some as inaction—was created and nurtured by the Church. In any respect, some of the worst *and* best qualities of the Mexican character can be traced to religious origins."

Bandits & Dictators

Prior to the arrival of the Spanish *conquistadores*, the Aztecs and most of the other inhabitants of Mexico lived in hierarchically arranged authoritarian regimes administered by hereditary kings, chiefs and priests.

Virtually every area of life was strictly controlled by detailed laws and taboos that were harshly enforced. The Aztecs believed that regular human sacrifices, often on a massive scale, were necessary to keep the sun rising every day and the rest of the cosmos in proper working order.

Most of the victims sacrificed to the gods were enemies captured for that specific purpose. But special ceremonies called for the immolation of their own people, including children who were specially raised for sacrificial purposes. In other words, there were many similarities in the religious and political philosophies and practices of the conquering Spaniards and their Mexican Indian prisoners of war.

The first tragedy of the Spanish conquest of Mexico was, in fact, unintended. Alien diseases brought into the country by the *conquistadores* nearly wiped out the huge Indian population. The second tragedy was the deliberate attempt by the Spaniards to totally obliterate the cultures of the Indians and remake them in the image of themselves—a policy that brought untold suffering to the Indians because it destroyed their spiritual as well as their physical world and left them in profound cultural shock.

A third tragedy was that the Spaniards were congenitally unable to accept the surviving Indians of Mexico as fully sentient human beings who had as much right to freedom and the pursuit of happiness as they did.

Because of this attitude the Spanish administrators of colonial Mexico treated the Indians as chattel to be used as they saw fit; or as irritants who were in the way and were to be ignored or eliminated, depending on the circumstances.

Still another tragedy was the political role played by the Roman Catholic Church of Mexico during the 300-year Spanish regime and the following 100 years of autocratic rule by military despots. The Church conspired with the military and the Spanish-descended elite of the country to keep both the Indians and Mestizos of Mexico ignorant, politically powerless and in a state of permanent poverty.

The laws of the country were designed to keep the secular and ecclesiastical elite in power at the expense of the poor. The justice system was used by those in power to preserve the status quo and to enrich themselves.

This heritage of political powerlessness, poverty and abuse of the common people—which did not really begin to end until the mid-1900s—became an indelible part of the character and spirit of the disenfranchised people of Mexico, imbuing them with a capacity for extraordinary patience and endurance, and an even greater capacity for violence when they could no longer endure.

Most Mexicans today are still mired in poverty, but political awareness and political activism on every level of society, combined with a new breed of democratic and reform-minded leaders, is slowly but surely wrenching the country up and out of the muck of its colonial and dictatorial past.

Slaves, Serfs & Poverty
Once the Spanish conquerors of Mexico had consolidated their control of the central portions of the former Aztec empire, the Spanish Court divided the country up into territorial fiefs and agricultural estates called *encomiendas* (en-coh-me-ENN-dahs), gave some of them to the conquering *conquistadores* and

friends of the Court, and sold or leased others to high-born Spaniards.

These land grants included all of the Indians who lived in the areas concerned. Laws were then passed requiring the Indians to pay tribute in money or kind to the grant holders, based on a percentage of everything they produced. The Indians were also required to work directly for the landlords as serfs and laborers, usually for their keep.

In the mid-1500s huge deposits of silver were discovered in several locations in central Mexico. Thereafter, large numbers of Indians were forced to work 12 or more hours a day in the mines. At night they were chained or locked up in pens to pre-vent them from running away.

Racked by a variety of diseases, ill-fed and treated brutally by their overseers, the Indian mine workers died by the thou-sands. Eventually there were not enough Indian laborers to meet the demand, so mining companies began using Mestizos and black slaves brought in from Africa.

During the first 200 years or so of the Spanish period Mexico's burgeoning population of Mestizos could not engage in any of the professions, and were relegated to menial jobs or no work at all. In the cities many mixed-bloods lived as scavengers and thieves. In the countryside many became bandits, creating a virtually lawless environment. For most of the 300 years of the Spanish era in Mexico Indians could not hold title to land or own or ride horses.

During the latter decades of the Spanish period hundreds of thousands of Indians were landless and homeless, wandering the countryside and cities as vagrants.

However, by the third century of the Spanish period in Mexico, small numbers of urban Mestizos had become crafts-men, clerks and shopkeepers. In the northern regions where cattle and sheep raising had grown into a major industry, many Mestizos had become *vaqueros* (vah-KAY-rohs) or horsemen, and had begun to develop a consciousness and an identity that would eventually play a leading role in the creation of the mod-ern state of Mexico.

Both Indians and Mestizos played significant roles in the Mexican war for independence from 1810 to 1821, but neither the Indians nor the vast majority of the Mestizos gained anything from the victory over Spain.

For yet another 100 years over 90 percent of all Mexicans remained frozen in time—dominated by the Church, the military and the government; mostly illiterate, and scrabbling to stay alive as peons and factory workers who were little more than slaves.

During the 1800s it was common for factory owners—many of whom were Americans and Europeans—to pay their workers in script that could only be spent at company-owned stores. Some paid their workers in mescal, a potent alcoholic drink made from the agave cactus.

These conditions led to Mexico's revolutionary war of 1910-1921, which primarily pitted the landless peasants and their few allies against the huge estate-holding land-lords, the corporate barons, the higher echelons of the Catholic Church, and their mercenary armies.

This was the war in which Mestizo bandits like Pancho Villa and peasant revolutionaries like Emiliano Zapata drenched Mexico in fire and blood, finally ending the Church, state and military cabal that had ruled the country so ruthlessly for four centuries.

The victors in the revolution immediately began implementing plans to divide the great landed estates among the peons who actually worked them, to bring public education to the masses, and to remedy the worst abuses of the labor system in the country.

Enormous progress has been made since the end of the great war in 1921, but there is still a long way to go. The reforms and improvements have barely touched the bulk of the Indians of Mexico, and nearly half of all other Mexicans still live in or close to the poverty level. This legacy of economic hardship and abuse is another of the key factors in the crucible of history that shaped the character and personality of today's rural and poor urban Mexicans.

The wonder of it is that Mexicans are not more bitter and resentful than they are, and how, despite such a legacy, the majority of Mexicans are kind, thoughtful, generous, and have an extraordinarily sunny disposition that is volubly expressed in art, literature, music and song.

The Social Heritage
A key part of the character and personality of present-day Mexicans naturally evolved from social attitudes and behavior they inherited from both their Spanish

and Indian forbearers. Prior to the arrival of the Spanish *conquistadores* in 1519, the Aztecs and other Indians of Mexico, despite the more inhuman aspects of their religious practices, were dedicated artists, poets, musicians, singers and dancers. All Aztec youths were professionally trained in dancing and singing, and large numbers were trained as musicians.

Festivals, which revolved around magnificent floral and graphic displays, costumes, music, minutely choreographed dancing, recitations and singing, were an integral part of the lives of the Aztecs and other Mexican Indians. There were numerous regular occasions at which eating and drinking were especially designed to satisfy all the senses of the mind and body.

Sex, although carefully regulated to support the existence of the family unit, was recognized and celebrated as one of the special pleasures of life. There was organized gambling as well as numerous aesthetic practices, along with spectator and participation sports and other forms of recreation.

At the same time, the Indian societies of Mexico were authoritarian and hierarchal, with responsibilities and privileges determined by family lineage, social rank and other factors. Personal relations and etiquette were based on rank, sex, position and age, and were highly refined and strictly enforced.

It is amply recorded that the Aztecs and other Mexican Indians had a rich philosophical, emotional and spiritual life; that they had a sometimes macabre but always funny sense of humor, and delighted in jokes and storytelling.

And then came the Spanish *conquistadores*, Catholic missionaries, colonial administrators, soldiers, and over-seers, who took it upon themselves to destroy the Indian cultures and replace them with their own—a daunting task that obviously did not faze the Spaniards, coming as it did, at the end of seven centuries of effort to retake Spain from its Moorish invaders.

Although this attempt to convert Mexico's Indian population was only partially successful, the Spanish influence on the surviving Indians was profound. The Indians went from being a relatively prosperous and joyous people to being passive, almost mute, servants, serfs and slaves whose lives were filled with frustration and sadness.

The sophisticated etiquette, social rituals and macho complex that the *conquistadores*, clergy, and colonial administrators brought from Spain were transplanted in Mexico intact and then elaborated on as the generations went by.

For the Spanish overlords of Mexico the long colonial era was mostly a golden age. Within two generations, exports from newly discovered silver mines and huge plantations and haciendas had created a wealthy class that was able to spend most of its time in the pursuit of pleasure.

Courting rituals, bullfights, exhibitions of horseback riding and rodeo skills, cockfights, festivals, banquets and gambling filled the lives of the Spanish colonials, creating a culture that was far removed from the lives of the Mestizos and Indians.

Following the Mexican war for independence in 1810-21, more and more Mestizos began to adopt the culture created by the Spanish colonials, absorbing their attitudes and etiquette, and imitating their lifestyles in every way they could. But the poorer and more frustrated the Mestizos were, the more they emphasized the macho behavior of the Spaniards, particularly their attitude toward women in general and their treatment of their girl friends, wives and children.

From their Indian side, the Mestizos of Mexico had inherited a superstitious nature, a deep respect for the spiritual side of life, tolerance for things they could not change, the ability to endure hardship, patience, and extraordinary dignity.

The overall social position of Mexico's Mestizo population improved only slightly following the war for independence from Spain in 1810-21. It was not until the Mexican revolution of 1910-21 that Mestizos, by then the overwhelming majority in the country, began to recognize themselves as a new race and to win some of the rights of full citizenship.

This sense of the hybrid people of Mexico being a new race was advanced and popularized by philosopher-writer Jose Vasconcelos who became education minister in the new revolutionary government. He referred to Mestizos as *la raza* (lah rah-zah), or "the race," by which he meant all Latin-Americans who were born of mixed Spanish and Indian parentage.

In Vasconcelos' definition, members of *la raza* were a superior group of people because they were a merger of many of the best attributes of the Indians and the Spanish. But this new arbitrary label was only a distant dream and did not still the hearts and souls of most Mestizos because it was meaningless to them. They continued to suffer from discrimination and to be plagued by doubts of their legitimacy as a people and their ability to meet others on an equal footing.

Mestizos account for close to 80 percent of the population of present-day Mexico, and most have not yet overcome their legacy of self-doubt. (Indians make up around 15 percent of Mexico's population, about four percent are pure European in blood, and the rest are racially African and Asian).

Humility and Arrogance

Until the final decade of the 20th century most Mexicans looked upon the U.S. as an arrogant and aggressive nation, with good reason, and many still do.

Soon after American settlers in the Texas portion of the Mexican state of Coahuila rebelled in the 1830s and declared the region an independent nation, the United States invaded Mexico and annexed the entire northern portion of the country (including what is now New Mexico, Arizona, California and part of Colorado), reducing its national territory by approximately one half.

Throughout most of the rest of the 1800s a number of American politicians and newspapers advocated publicly and loudly that the U.S. should take the rest of Mexico as well.

There were no more full-fledged military invasions of Mexico by the United States,* but between the 1870s and the beginning of the Mexican revolutionary war in 1910 American (and European) business barons owned and controlled a significant proportion of all manufacturing and production in Mexico.

Most of these American and European businessmen tolerated and supported working conditions in their Mexican factories and farms that were reminiscent of the early centuries of the Spanish colonial period when Mexican Indians and Mestizos were treated like slaves and beasts of burden.

In 1911 the American government repeatedly ordered U.S. warships into Mexican ports in the Gulf of Mexico in actions designed to influence the outcome of the Mexican revolutionary war that had started the previous year. Finally, in 1914, the U.S. Navy bombarded and temporarily occupied the port of Veracruz. At that time, the U.S. had contingency plans to invade and occupy Mexico City but the plans were not carried out because successes of the Mexican rebels preempted the American invasion plans.

Throughout this period and on up until the 1960s and 970s Mexicans who lived along the U.S. border, and Mexican-Americans on the U.S. side of the border, were routinely discriminated against and physically abused. Many were killed by Americans who were never arrested or charged for their crimes.

Michael T. Eakins, a bilingual American businessman with years of experience in Mexico, notes: "Mexicans, much to their chagrin, have long been economically dependent upon the United States for tourism, trade and investment, resulting in a love-hate relationship,"

Time has healed most of the worst wounds Mexicans have suffered at the hands of Americans, and the level of the friction between the two countries continues to decrease. But Mexicans are still sensitive about the aggressiveness and perceived arrogance of Americans, making it important for U.S. business-people doing business with Mexicans to be on their best behavior.

Mexican society itself has traditionally been mark-ed by extremes of arrogance and humility that were primarily determined by social class and sexual gender. Those with political and economic power have typically behaved in an arrogant manner toward the poor and powerless. Men have typically treated wo-men in an arrogant manner as part of their masculine posture.

Generally, the more powerful the Mexican indivi-dual or organization, the more arrogant the behavior. Until the 1920s the Catholic Church was the most powerful organization in Mexico. It conditioned the poor to behave humbly but itself behaved with su-preme arrogance and condoned arrogance among the rich and the politically powerful. With the exception of a few years in the mid-1800s, the government was informally and formally allied with the Church, exercised absolute power over ordinary people and treated them with arrogance as well as callous indifference.

To those in power, arrogance—often combined with brutality—came with the territory. To the powerless, humility and passivity was their only security against reprisals from both the state and the Church. Not being able to influence either the Church or the state or otherwise defend themselves, the power-less men of Mexico frequently turned their frustrations and anger inward onto themselves, their families, and often innocent bystanders as well.

After the choke-hold that the Catholic Church had on Mexico was finally severed in the 1920s and new generations of bishops and priests took over, the attitudes and behavior of the Church gradually changed from that of an oppressor to being an advocate of the rights of the people.

By the 1980s the Church was no longer the evil overlord that it had once been, and the poor people of Mexico had begun to think for themselves for the first time in the history of the country. But the passivity and humility instilled into the poor by the Church for so many generations has not yet run its course and still today often has a powerfully negative effect on the character and personality of ordinary Mexican employees.

The revolution against the political dictatorship that began in Mexico in 1910 is said by many intellectuals to still be in progress. Tremendous strides have been made since the 1920s, and particularly since the 1980s, but the legacy of a government based on ignoring human and democratic rights for more than 400 years is very much alive.

Transforming Mexico into a fully democratic and humane society requires more than legislation and political posturing. It requires a variety of changes that get down to the cultural roots of the Mexican character.

Until that happens, foreigners doing business in Mexico must learn how to deal with the twin factors of arrogance and humility that continue to complicate inter-personal relationships and set Mexicans apart.

Race, Caste and Class

Until modern times in Mexico, race, birthplace, and family history generally determined one's social class and fortune. From the first decades of the Spanish period in Mexico, which began in 1521, there were basically three classes of people: pure Spanish who were born in Spain; pure Spanish who were born in Mexico, and Mexican Indians.

Wholesale miscegenation by the early Spanish *Conquistadores*, colonial administrators and Spanish military garrisons with Indian women—and later black female slaves—brought about a dramatic evolutionary change in the social and class system during the first century of the colonization of Mexico.

The *conquistadores* and other Spaniards who followed them were extremely conscious of name, race and class distinctions. They became even more concerned about these factors as the number of mixed-bloods spiraled upward, making it even more important for them to distinguish themselves from the lower classes.

By the second century there were so many different racial mixtures that the Spanish authorities created a total of 16 different racial categories, providing the foundation for a caste system that was to endure until the end of the Spanish period in 1821. [Some of the categories were so absurd they became the subject of macabre humor.]

This meticulous categorizing of people by their racial ancestry contributed enormously to the division of the people of Mexico into precise classes. Those who were pure Spanish were at the top of the social ladder and Indians were at the bottom. This caste system made it very important for families in the higher social classes to maintain careful records of their ancestry.

As in all old societies at that time, there were certain Spanish families that became successful in earlier generations and passed on to their descendants' names that were illustrious to varying degrees. Upper class people followed the custom of using two last names—the paternal family name and the ma-ternal family name, with the paternal name coming before the maternal name. In other words, in the name Juan Carrera Cortes, Carrera is the paternal name and Cortes is the maternal name.

The paternal name is used when addressing some-one directly. In this case, Señor Carrera.

While names themselves are no longer the only passport to the upper class or indicative of an elite status, racial mixture and class are still key factors in Mexican society. Generally speaking social and economic status in present-day Mexico have a direct correlation with racial color. The darker people are the more likely they are to be in the lower class; and vice versa, lighter-skinned people make up the bulk of the middle and upper classes.

Upper and middle-class Mexicans typically say there is no racial or color discrimination in the country. But it is built into the psyche of the people and is reflected in every facet of society, from marriage preferences to hiring preferences. The higher one goes on the social and economic scale, the more prominent color preferences become.

Those who say that racial and color prejudices do not exist in Mexico are usually thinking only in terms of mixing in public places, where the rainbow of colors do, in fact, mix with little or no apparent friction.

Whatever the circumstances, foreign business-people should be sensitive to the issue of skin color in Mexico not only because it does impact on business at a higher level but also in order to avoid discriminating against anyone.

Other legacies that Mexicans inherited from their extra-ordinary past include their overall intellectual and spiritual view of them-selves and the world at large—much of which has traditionally been negative. In the words of one Mexican businessman, "Hernan Cortes and the Spanish viceroys still rule in Mexico. We are plagued by our past, and will not be able to achieve our potential until we can finally put it to rest."

(2)
INTELLECTUAL
&
SPIRITUAL MEXICO

The Role of Aesthetics

Until the last two decades of the 20th century, ordinary Americans and other foreigners were inclined to view Mexicans as intellectually unsophisticated and spiritually backward. This image, based on ignorance as well as prejudice, was totally false. In reality, most Mexicans, including those with minimal education, have an enormous store of cultural wisdom, pro-found spiritual beliefs that go well beyond Christian theology, and have traditionally enjoyed a quality of life that was not dependent upon affluence or book learning.

One of the most important facets of the combined spiritual and intellectual side of Mexicans is their highly developed aesthetic sense, most of which they owe to their Indian ancestors who lived close to nature and drew their inspiration from the earth and the heavens.

Like virtually all ancient people, Mexican Indians believed that all things in nature—not just man—have a spirit that should be respected, and in some cases worshipped. Nature, in all of its marvelous simplicity, set the standards by which they measured aesthetic qualities. To them, the ultimate in manmade beauty was a depiction of nature imbued with spirit.

Present-day Mexicans are still culturally imbued with this aesthetic sensitivity, and it is reflected—albeit invisibly to most outsiders—in virtually every facet of their lives.

The Importance of Art

A constant need for spiritual security and satisfaction inspired Mexican Indians to create images and structures of beauty to serve and please the spirits, making art an integral part of their physical, intellectual and emotional lives. In this animistic world of the Indians art was not created for its own sake. It was a symbol of the spiritual world and a method of communicating with the spirits that was vital to the survival of the people.

This spiritually oriented artistic legacy remains visible in present-day Mexico, not only in the artifacts of the past but also in contemporary murals, sculptures and other art forms, and still today speaks with a powerful voice that stirs the Mexican soul.

Virtually every region in Mexico has been noted for centuries for its special arts and handicrafts, from metal ware and pottery to woodcarvings. Some kind of handicraft production has traditionally been the sole industry in many villages. But veteran Mexican hand Dirk Weisheit says this artistic heritage is in danger of being eroded away by creeping industrialization and adoption of Western values.

It may, in fact, be too much to hope that political and economic reforms now underway in Mexico will preserve and encourage the artistic impulse that has been so much a part of the Mexican psyche.

First generation Mexican-Americans and Mexicans who are in the U.S. on work permits often say that one of the things they miss most about Mexico is the abundance of art in Mexican life. American anthropologist-author Marilyn P. Davis quotes Mexican muralist Victor Orozco Ochoa in *Mexican Voices/ American Dreams* [Henry Holt] as saying that what the U.S. needs to help stem violence among the young is more artists; not more policemen. Orozco says that expressing oneself through art sublimates the tendency for mischief and violence that afflicts those who feel frustrated.

American businessman Jack Scott, founder and chairman of the board of Key International, agrees. He notes: "Some years ago I arranged with the State of Jalisco for a cultural exchange with Arizona. This included bringing some paintings, by such artists as Orozcos, Tamayos and Sequieros, that had never before allowed outside of Mexico to be exhibited at the Phoenix Art Musuem, along with a collection of arts and crafts from *Casa de los Artisanias de Jalisco* for display in the Phoenix Public Library.

"We also brought the 40-plus-member *Ballet Folklorico de Jalisco* which performed three afternoons in local high schools and in the evenings in the patio of the library. The reception at Central High School (predominately Hispanic) was a three-hour standing ovation. Other than the popular Mexican Hat Dance, few if any of the students had seen typical Jalisco dances or heard the regional music of Mexico.

"They were completely unaware of the beauty of Mexican dances and the traditions they represent. The students kept cheering and the dancers kept dancing. Finally the performance had to be stopped so the dancers could get to the library on time for the evening show. But once the group got to the library, the feet of several of the dancers were so swollen and they had so many blisters they couldn't go on.

"The principal of Central High reported that for several weeks after the performance at the school there was a conspicuously favorable change in the attitude and behavior of the Hispanic students. He attributed this change to a new pride in their Mexican heritage."

Among Mexico's greatest painters: Jose Clemente Orozco, Diego Rivera and David Alfaro Siqueiros.

The Importance of Music & Song
In the pre-Columbian world of Mexico playing musical instruments and singing were among the primary means of communicating with the spiritual entities who ruled the earth and the affairs of man. Practically all of the religious rituals of the Aztecs and other Indian nations of Mexico revolved around music, singing and dancing, and were inseparable from them. In every Aztec community there was a *Cuicacuilli*, or "House of Song" where the young were taught to sing and to perform ritual dances as an integral part of their education. Attending the "houses of song" was mandatory.

The Spanish fortune hunters who conquered Mexico in 1519-21, and the Catholic missionaries who quickly followed them, destroyed the houses of song and prohibited the surviving Indians (under their control) from performing any of their religious rituals.

But the Spaniards also brought with them their own traditions of music and singing, and as the generations went by these traditions flourished among the new race of Spanish-Indian Mestizos who were eventually to inherit the country.

Building on the bicultural traditions of their Indian and Spanish forbearers, this new race of Mexicans made music and song into an important part of their lifestyle, taking it well beyond its religious origins.

European visitors to Mexico during the middle years of the Spanish colonial regime (1521-1821) made special note of the role of music in the country, saying that playing music and singing seemed to be in the soul of Mexicans.

Mexico's growing population of Spanish-Indian mixtures, virtual outcasts from both Spanish and Indian societies during the colonial period, had, in fact, resorted to music, singing and dancing not only for spiritual solace but also for emotional release from the hardships and abuse inflicted upon them by the colonial regime and the Catholic Church.

While Mexico's traditions of music and song have suffered from the increased pace of industrialized life, enough of the traditions remain that they continue to add a special and very seductive ingredient to contemporary Mexican culture. Everyone who spends even a few days in Mexico, for whatever purpose, invariably encounters the ongoing Mexican love-affair with music, singing and dancing.

In addition to whatever personal enjoyment foreign busi-nesspeople might derive from being exposed to the musical traditions of Mexico, it is important that they understand and appreciate the role that music plays in the overall emotional and spiritual health of the people. Rather than view the Mexican penchant for musical entertainment as detracting from the work ethic, it should be regarded as an important factor in their wellbeing, and encouraged as a morale builder.

In fact, more and more Mexican-Americans are reconnecting with their cultural roots through music, and an appreciation for the Latin touch is quickly seeping into Anglo American society as well. The growing popularity of Mexican-American singers and bands throughout the United States is a significant testimony to the increasing bi-cultural sophistication of Americans in general.

The Importance of Literature

Another of the cultural legacies that educated modern-day Mexicans inherited from both their Indian and Spanish ancestors is a high regard for literature. ("Less educated Mexicans read comic books!"—Dirk Weisheit.)

In both medieval Spain and pre-Columbian Mexico, the use of language for religious purposes in particular contributed to the development of poetry and the appearance of literature in general.

The Aztecs, along with the savage and gruesome sides of their culture, typically thought, spoke and wrote in poetic terms that added a conspicuously metaphysical, uplifting quality to their lives.

Because literature was so closely related to both religion and government in Spain and Mexico, it occupied an important place in the lives of the Spanish conquistadors and the Mexican Indians they sub-jugated. During and following the Spanish colonial regime in Mexico, the omnipresent all powerful Catholic Church sustained the role of ecclesiastical literature, and predisposed formally educated Mexicans to having a deep-seated interest in all of the forms of literature that began appearing just prior to the revolutionary war in 1910-21.

The first writings of Mexico's Mestizos—the once despised and oppressed race that had become the majority by the beginning of the revolution—were especially popular among those who were well enough educated to read because, for the first time in their history, someone was speaking in their voice for them.

A significant number of present-day Mexicans have retained this interest in literature, sometimes to the point that it verges on an obsession. Passionate discussions of topics raised by writers make up an important facet of the lives of middle and upper class intellectuals.

In fact, most educated Mexicans automatically play the role of universal philosophers, enthusiastically holding forth on any subject that comes up, and one has to be pretty well read to keep up with them.

Foreign businesspeople who are not well-grounded in English literature, much less Mexican literature, past as well as present, may find themselves disad-vantaged in their efforts to develop the personal relationships that are essential for success in Mexico.

At the very least, businesspeople headed for Mexico should read the books of half a dozen or so of Mexico's most famous writers and poets (generally available in English translations), know the names of some of the country's great artists, and be familiar with the names and thinking of some of the current social scientists and economists. (As for some of Mexico's most influential economists, Mexican-American businessman Walter J. Gomez recommends Luis Pazos and Alberto Barranco Chavarria.)

On the literary front, a number of Hispanic writers, particularly several Hispanic female writers living in the U.S., should be on any "Must Read" list of books about Latin thinking and behavior. In the 1980s and early 1990s several of these *Latina* (Lah-TEE-nah) writers were "discovered" by mainstream publishing in the U.S., and are now recognized as literary lionesses, speaking with voices that had been stilled for centuries behind the iron doors of the Catholic Church and the cult of machoism.

The soul-searing eloquence of some of these writers is so powerful it leaves the reader stunned, causing one to go back and read some of the scenes over and over again to savor the fullness of their anger, their passion, and their love. Four of this new breed of *Latina* writers who have been singled out for special praise are Julia Alvarez, Denise Chavez, Sandra Cisneros, and Ana Castillo.

Among their most notable books:

In the Time of the Butterflies, Julia Alvarez (Algonquin Books).

Face of an Angel, Denise Chavez (Farrar, Straus and Giroux).

Loose Women, Sandra Cisneros (Alfred A. Knopf).

Massacre of the Dreamers: Essays in Xicanisma, Ana Castillo (University of New Mexico Press)

Another new voice of the Mexican female is that of Laura Esquivel, whose first novel *Like Water for Chocolate* (Anchor Books/Doubleday) became a national bestseller in both Mexico and the United States and was made into a successful movie that won 10 awards from the Mexican Academy of Motion Pictures.

My Mexican friends say that the funny, raunchy, sensual, poignant and magical *Like Water for Chocolate (Como Agua para Chocolate)* captures the essence of the mystical as well as the real-life of Mexicans and does more to explain Mexican psychology than most non-fiction works by professional authorities.

On the distaff side, another Mexican-American writer who has received high praise for his insightful books on the Mexican and Mexican-American experience is Victor Villaseñor, whose work includes *Macho* and *Rain of Gold* (Dell Publishing). The latter, a multi-generational history of Villaseñor's family, is widely regarded as a major classic on the order of Alex Haley's *Roots*.

Villaseñor's tale of gold, revolution, murder, rape, starvation and survival is a stunning testimony to the fortitude and resilience of the Indians and Mestizos of Mexico, and starkly reveals that over the generations it was the strength, courage and survival instincts of

Mexican mothers that saved the country and its culture from the darkest impulses of its hate-filled, angry men.

Business consultant Ronald C. Walker, who is headquartered in Puerto Vallarta, adds: "When recommending authors and books on Mexico, I always start with Octavio Paz and his classic book *The Labyrinth of Solitude* (New York, Grove and Weidenfeld). After more than two decades, I still consider it my Mexican bible."

Other philosopher-writers of note: Samual Ramos, Alfonso Reyes, Carlos Fuentes, Mariano Azuela, Juan Rulfo, Jorge Ibarguengoitia and Elena Poniatowska. Two of Mexico's most famous early poets: Sor Juana Ines de la Cruz (1648-1695) and Armado Nervo (1879-1919).

It is also helpful to know something about the metaphysical legacy Mexicans inherited from their Indian ancestors.

Mysticism and Myths
Mexico's pre-Columbian Indians saw the world as a spiritual manifestation that required constant awareness of the presence of spirits, regular communication with the more powerful gods, and strict obedience to their will in all things. These all-powerful spirits—not human beings—were the center of the Mexican universe, and shaped the lives of the people.

It was this spiritual image of the world that prompted Moctezuma, emperor of the Aztecs, to literally hand his crown over to Hernan Cortes and his band of *conquistadores* when they arrived in the Aztecan capital in 1519.

Moctezuma believed Cortes was an ancient Aztec king who had come back to life as a god to reclaim his throne. This tragic event was the prelude to the total destruction of the Aztec empire, and eventually led to the death of more than 80 percent of the Indian population of Mexico through slaughter, abuse and disease.

The conquering Spaniards did their best to destroy the spiritual world of the Indians who survived the conquest by killing most of their priests, destroying their temples and sacred books, prohibiting them from practicing their traditional religious rites, then attempting to impose Catholicism upon them. Ultimately, the Spaniards failed to completely destroy the culture of the surviving Indians because they kept them segregated outside of Spanish society.

Over the 300 years of the Spanish regime the Indians gradually absorbed some of the tenets and rituals of Catholicism, but they did not give up their own beliefs, and eventually fused the two together.

Indianized Catholicism
Describing present-day Mexico—or any country—as a "Catholic" country is misleading if not a misnomer, depending on one's definition of what it means to be Catholic. For most people, the label of "Catholic" is little more than a convenient tag. In any event, the Catholicism brought to Mexico by the Spanish conquistadors and their missionary camp-followers was soon hybridized to make it more acceptable to the subjugated Indians.

In addition to recasting Mary, the mother of Jesus Christ, in the image of an Indian woman (*Nuestra Señora de Guadalupe* or Our Lady of Guadalupe), and making Tepeyac (now in Mexico City) the equivalent of Jerusalem, many of the rituals of the Church were eventually altered to accommodate traditional beliefs and customs of the native inhabitants.

As more than one cynic has observed, the Catholic Church not only absorbed most of Mexico's Indians into its body by first denying them the right to practice their own religions and then baptizing them, it also baptized and absorbed some of their gods as well.*

---

*"This was typical of the early Catholic Church's efforts to destroy the native religions throughout Latin America. In Haiti, for example, pictures of Mary were used to replace icons of Erzulla, the goddess of oceans and streams. An icon of Jesus Christ was used to replace Damballah, god of the forests and fertility. Pictures of Catholic saints were substituted for lesser gods. In Brazil, the god Macumba was replaced with a Christian image"—Jack Scott, Key International.

Thus while Mexico's Spanish-Indian Mestizos and most of its pureblooded Indians were coated with a patina of Roman Catholicism and the culture that came with the Spanish language, the coating was little more than skin-deep, particularly as far as the Indians were concerned.

What was of special importance, however, was the fact that Mestizos who lived in urban areas under direct Spanish influence, also absorbed Spanish etiquette and a great deal of the ethics of their Spanish overlords—a phenomenon that was to have a profound impact on the future of the country.

But despite the cultural impact that Spain had on Mexico the spirits of both Indians and Mixtures remained Indian, and it is this *Indianism* that is responsible for the many parallels between Mexican and Oriental attitudes and behavior, particularly in the country's business etiquette and ethics.

Creating a Separate Reality

By the end of the Spanish regime in Mexico in 1821 male Mestizos had created a new reality for themselves. From their Indian side they had taken a heavy dose of mysticism, stoicism and patience. From their Spanish side they had absorbed an exaggerated form of machoism, a stylized etiquette, an extraordinary sensitivity to any kind of real or imagined slight, and a tendency to be callous and cruel.

The virtual reality created by this new race of Mexican men was designed to provide them with the things that the real world did not—pride, respect, order and security. But in fact it was a world filled with frustration and often senseless violence that remains common in Mexican society today.

Freedom from Spain in 1821, from home-grown dictators in 1917, and partial freedom from the yoke of the Church in the following decade, brought some relief to the formerly outcast Mestizos, but nothing at all to the Indians. The country remained in the hands of a small elite group that continued most of the political and economic abuses of the past.

Efforts to bring about across-the-board deep-seated reforms in Mexico's traditionally exploitive political and economic systems did not really begin until the Carlos Salinas administration in 1988 and the Ernesto Zedillo Administration of 1994. But still today there is a *Remote Mexico* that is a continuation of the past and a *Near Mexico* that represents the promise of the future.

Remote Mexico is inhabited by Indians who mostly live in the southern states under conditions that have changed little since colonial times, and by the urban and rural poor Mestizos who exist at close to the subsistence level. Together these two groups account for close to half of the Mexican population.

Near Mexico is made up of a moderately well-to-do group that makes up the bulk of the commercial and professional class, and a small elite group of politically connected, wealthy families that control most of the country's assets.

Early hopes that reforms initiated by President Carlos Salinas during his administration (1988-1994) and by his successor President Ernesto Zedillo (1994-2000) would result in dramatic improvements in both the political and economic spheres were dashed by a financial collapse in 1995 and a number of high-level scandals and assassinations. Both Salinas and Zedillo came into office like white knights, but as had traditionally been the rule in Mexico they soon lost their image of saviors and came under severe criticism from most Mexicans.

Notes Michael T. Eakins, a specialist in marketing in Mexico: "Had it not been for the economic austerity programs implemented by President Miguel de la Madrid during his presidency (1982-1988), President Salinas would not have been in a position to implement most of his reform programs in the first place.

"Furthermore, while President Salinas can be given credit for an aggressive privatization program which attracted massive foreign investment, and made admirable efforts to clean up such institutions as the Customs Bureau and labor unions, he also positioned himself to become one of the primary benefactors of these programs, and left office as one of the richer men in the world."

Most ordinary Mexicans who live in *Near Mexico* have not given up hope, however. They still believe that combining the intellectual and spiritual legacy of their past with a less emotional and more rational approach to business and life in general will bring both order and prosperity to Mexico.

It is this group of people, still in the throes of a cultural, political and economic revolution, who are interfacing with the outside world in Mexico's international affairs. And it is their etiquette and ethics that foreigners must cope with to do business successfully with Mexico.

(3)
THE MEXICAN
CHARACTER TODAY

Cultural Regions of Mexico

Just as Mexico is geographically diverse, with high, dry plains, deserts, great mountain ranges, wet, lush jungles and tropical beaches, there are also pronounced cultural differences. Six major regions are recognized by both social scientists and the business community. From north to south, these regions are:

1) The long but narrow swath of northern Mexico that borders the United States and is known as the Border Region.
2) The wide band that is just south of the border zone and is known as the Northern Region.
3) The Western Central Region.
4) Mexico City and its environs.
5) The Southern Region.
6) Yucatan.

The Border Region is marked by the cities of Tijuana, Nogales, Agua Prieta, Ciudad Juarez, Piedras Negras, Nuevo Laredo and Matamoros, its free-zone foreign-owned factories (the much-touted *maquiladoras* / mah-kee-lah-DOH-rahs), its large number of immigrants from the interior of Mexico, and old-time residents who have been partly Americanized.

The Northern Region consists of the rest of the border states of Sonora, Chihuahua, Coahuila, Nuevo Leon and Tamaulipas, and the northern portions of Durango. Monterrey, Mexico's third largest city, is considered the center of this region. The Northern Region has traditionally been regarded as Mexico's frontier, and the equivalent of the U.S. West during the 1800s.

Mexicans who settled in this area from around 1600—Mexican-born Spaniards and Spanish-Indian Mestizos—were pioneers who created cattle ranches and the profession of the cowboy.

Some of the Mestizos who moved into this region from Mexico City and other central metropolitan areas became cattle rustlers and gunfighters, and in later generations, revolutionaries as well. *Nortenos* (Nohr-TAY-nyohs) or "Northerners," as residents of this region are called, are still known for their independent spirit, aggressive ways, strong work ethic and equally strong political views (most of Mexico's revolutionary generals and later presidents were from this region).

Not surprisingly, *Nortenos* are also known for their sometimes vehement dislike of people from Mexico City, whom they disparagingly refer to as *Chilangos* (Chee-LAHN-gohs).* The main reason for this enmity is that people in this region have traditionally believed that Mexico City residents got an unfair share of all tax revenues and other government benefits, while they were generally ignored.

---

*There are several stories about the origin of *chilango* and its use as a derogatory term referring to residents of Mexico City. The most likely of these stories (according to Professor Daniel Arreola of the Center for Latin American Studies, Arizona State University) is that it originated in the gulf port city of Veracruz as a corruption of the word *wachinango* (wah-chee-NAHN-go) which means "red snapper" (the fish). After Veracruz became famous as a recreational area, large numbers of fair-skinned people from Mexico City began flocking to its beaches, and ended up getting burned red by its hot sun. At first local people began referring to these people as *wachinangos* or "red snappers." Eventually this was shortened to *chilango* and came to mean any person who lived in Mexico City.

The Western Central Region, which centers around Guadalajara, the capital of Jalisco and Mexico's second largest city, can probably best be described culturally as the birthplace of the country's famous *mariachi* music, the Hat Dance, tequila, and the upper class Mexican cowboy, or *chorro* (CHOH-roh).

Although Guadalajara has gone from being noted primarily for its agriculture and small, family-owned business to being a center of industrial enterprise, the people have maintained most of their laid-back, fun-loving character that is subsumed in the word *Tapatios* (Tah-pah-TEE-ohs) traditionally used in reference to the residents of the region. (The term is said to be from an old Indian phrase that means "Three times worthy.")

Mexico City, the fourth region and the world's largest city, is the economic, political and cultural center of Mexico. Virtually a country within itself, *La Capital* (Lah Cah-pee-TAHL) represents everything that is good and bad about the country, from enormous wealth and the etiquette of a refined culture to the most abject poverty and violence.

Affluent residents of Mexico City are as sophisticated as their counterparts in any major world capital, "but they are not 'international' like the residents of Brussels, Hong Kong, New York, etc." says Dirk Weisheit. The business culture remains Mexican in practically every sense of the word, including a thick layer of bureaucracy that adds its own nuance to getting things done.

Mexico's Southern Region is made up of the states of Oaxaca, Chiapas and all of the Yucatan Peninsula, where the majority of the inhabitants are full-blooded Indians and where things have changed very little—socially, economically or politically—in the past hundred years.

The region is dominated by large landowners who run their banana and coffee plantations like small fiefdoms, and by local bosses who are the modern-day equivalents of the *caciques* (cah-CEE-kehs) or chiefs of pre-Columbian Mexico. Foreigners who have had extensive business experience in this region say it is like another country.

There are also a number of smaller geographic and cultural "pockets" in Mexico where there are distinctive local attitudes and customs that impact on the way business is done.

Notes Dirk Weisheit: "Mexican-Americans and Mexicans from the border zone, especially those who claim to be gringos, are very different from Mexicans who live in Mexico City and other interior regions of the country. These people are generally viewed as untrustworthy and are almost never fully accepted in *La Capital*. Doors to the most influential people in Mexico can usually be opened by heavyweight gringos after a lot of effort, but only rarely by *pochos* (POH-chohs)* or 'Americanized Mexicans who live along the border'."

*The original meaning of *pocho* (POH-choh) is something that has been soiled or spoiled by discoloration.

Despite the many regional differences in the character of Mexicans, all share a core character that is one of the common legacies of their unique history. Adds business consultant Ronald C. Walker: "In my opinion, it is a common mistake for Americans to assume that Mexico is becoming more Americanized as more and more American style products appear in the country and more Mexicans dress like Americans and learn how to speak English. In my view, the reality—or a separate reality—is that Mexicans are performing a ritual that they have been practicing for centuries: physically adapting to out-side influences, while their thought processes and behavior remain virtually unchanged."

Personalismo
Coping With a Hostile World

Any understanding of the Mexican way of doing business must begin with the concept of *personalismo* (payr-soh-nah-LEES-moh) or "personalism." In fact, *personalismo* is the foundation of Mexican society. It grew out of the laws, policies and practices of the Spanish administrators and representatives of the Catholic Church who together ruled the country for 300 years, and is so deeply rooted in the culture that it routinely takes precedence over virtually everything else.

From the beginning of the Spanish era in 1521 until Mexican independence from Spain in 1821 the aim of the colonial administrators and the Church was to extract as much wealth from Mexico as possible.

Among other things, Spanish theologians had long before given their blessing to the practice of selling public offices to the highest bidders as a legitimate way of raising money for the Crown. These concepts and practices were brought to Mexico by the conquistadors.

The civil and ecclesiastical laws of colonial Mexico were primarily designed to protect and preserve those in power. The few laws that were aimed at protecting ordinary people were routinely ignored. Common people were forced to bow to the demands and whims of anyone who had any kind of official authority.

The revolution against Spain in 1810-1821 brought some improvements in the lives of a small percentage of the Mestizos, but socially, politically and economically most of them, particularly those who lived in rural areas, were to remain only one step above the Indians, mired in ignorance and poverty.

In this environment, ethics based on universal principles of right and wrong simply could not exist. All attitudes and behavior were controlled by arbitrarily created policies designed to protect and enrich the ruling elite, and by the personal agendas and whims of individuals in power.

All activity—social, economic and political—was based on personal relationships, on who one knew, or could get introductions to, and how much influence could be brought to bear on them. Equality, fairness and justice played no role in the economic and political spheres of life in Mexico. ("And still don't!"—Dirk Weisheit.)

This system put the burden of survival and success squarely on individuals, family groups and the networks they were capable of building in what was essentially a hostile environment. Anyone outside of one's own personal group was treated as a potential enemy or competitor, as someone to be taken advantage of, or ignored altogether, depending on the circumstances.

One of my contacts noted that entrepreneurs in Mexico have an especially difficult time. "If they aren't well-connected they can't get anywhere. This is especially true in any dealings with the government."

The only people who could thrive on their own in this hostile atmosphere were those in positions of authority because they could use their power to benefit themselves, their families and friends. Government officials, on all levels, were invariably the most selfish and ruthless in using their power for personal benefit.

Traditionally, everything in Mexico worked within a system of personalized patronage, from the highest echelons of government down to relationships between individuals. And some say that the reform programs announced to date are mostly public relations...that Mexico still has not changed that much.

Adds Key International's Jack Scott: "It is common for Mexicans to entice foreigners into taking them on as business associates, or soliciting remuneration, by announcing that they have a brother, uncle, cousin or other relative in an important government agency or ministry. Even if this is true, their influence may be minimal. Any such representation should be thoroughly checked out."

Moralidad
Dealing with Situational Ethics

Mexico's Nobel Prize-winning author-diplomat Octavio Paz said that traditional Mexican *moralidad* (moh-rah-lee-DAD) or "morality" was based on the ancient practice of patrimony in which rulers or chiefs treated domains and subjects as their private property.

In any event, proper behavior in its Mexican context was not based on a philosophical principle of right and wrong, but on inferiors demonstrating the "proper" kind and degree of respect, sincerity, and loyalty toward superiors in return for their support and favors.

Thus the height of traditional Mexican *moralidad* was to develop and nurture the personal relationships that were necessary to make this arbitrary, authoritarian system work. Within the context of this environment, one of the greatest sins was to commit an act that disturbed another person's emotional equilibrium or disrupted a personal relationship.

Because this system was based more on emotion than on intellect it was by nature extremely volatile. People had to exercise extraordinary care to avoid upsetting this fine balance even when they were among family and friends, particularly where male-female relations were concerned.

Personal violence became commonplace After the end of the Spanish regime in 1821 it was to take more than a century of vicious civil wars, police actions, political assassination and widespread banditry to dissipate most of the blood-lust that had built up during the Spanish period and the era of military dictators that followed.

It was not until the 1950s and 60s that large numbers of Mexican men stopped carrying weapons at all times and the volume of violence subsided to what is more or less normal for most societies.

Educated Mexicans have long been aware that situational ethics are an irrational and eventually destructive foundation for a society. But they were not been able to do very much about it because the entire political system was corrupt and was not about to reform itself. By the 1990s, however, a cadre of young politicians and bureaucrats, many of them educated abroad, had begun trying to undermine the power of the old guard and to cut away at the corruption that had flourished in the government since the Spanish era.

This process is continuing, but it will no doubt be at least another generation or two before most of the rot of the past can be exorcised from Mexican morality.

In 1995 Samuel del Villar, once an advisor to former President Miguel de la Madrid, wrote in an essay published by the Mexican daily *Reforma*: "The rules of modern civilization are democracy, justice, legality, efficiency and honesty. In Mexico the rules are tyranny, injustice, illegality, inefficiency, iresponsibility and decadence."

Fortunately, a small but growing number of Mexicans in business and in the government do make an effort to conduct themselves in a rational manner according to standards that are acceptable in the international community. Still today, however, the behavior of most Mexicans is determined by their relative positions within the vertical society, as opposed to any set of universal principles.

Individual Mexicans are incensed by aggressive, arrogant and corrupt behavior by others. But they are often forced to accept such behavior from people with whom they have a relationship because they depend on that person's goodwill and cooperation, and because they have been conditioned to accept such behavior as a natural prerogative of the other person's power.

Within the limiting confines of this system, personalized self-respect and dignity continue to take precedence over abstract or objective morality. Relationships and "face" continue to be the most important moral values.

But things are changing, primarily because of what *Business Week* magazine refers to as "the Zedillo Effect" in reference to reforms implemented by presidents Miguel de la Madrid (1988-1994) and Ernest Zedillo in 1994-2000. These reforms included privatization of state-owned industries, exposing corruption, purging corrupt officials from the ruling political party, and encouraging political pluralism.

But it will be a long time before the practice of morality in Mexico catches up with the concepts enumerated by Samuel del Villar.

As in the United States and elsewhere there are many facets of the moral values of Mexicans. For one thing, Mexico has its unscrupulous "scam artists"—some of whom specialize in victimizing foreign visitors. Their favorite targets seem to be foreign women and foreign men traveling alone because they are often the most vulnerable.

One of the earliest and most common scams frequently mentioned by expatriate residents in Mexico City: young shoe-shiners who quoted a low price then loudly demanded a vastly exaggerated sum when they finish, raising such a ruckus that a crowd gathers, resulting in the intimidated victims paying up.

This variety of scam artist is especially attracted to beach areas, and sometimes combine enough showman-ship with their acts that their "victims" do not complain. One who became notorious in Puerto Vallarta was a young boy who walked around carrying a live iguana, asking visitors if they would like to take his picture. As soon as the cameras clicked he demanded money.

(Of course, Puerto Vallarta itself had become famous as the location for the film *Night of the Iguana*, which starred Elizabeth Taylor, Ava Gardner and Richard Burton. After the filming, Burton and Taylor ended up getting married in the then isolated beach haven, and lived there for a while.)

An "official" scam that was long been common in Mexico was for police or uniformed military personnel to set up roadblocks, stop all motorists and hold them until they come up with a "gratuity." In some cases, these "roadblocks" were within a few yards of the Mexican-American border and were primarily aimed at tourists. In other cases, the roadblocks were in the interior of the country, and are aimed at farmers transporting their produce to local markets, wholesalers and exporters. Because much of the produce was perishable, the farmers could not afford to complain or get involved in delays of any kind, so they paid up.

Old-timers recommend that foreigners stopped by the police or uniformed personnel at roadblocks should *show* the police their driver's licenses if requested to do so, but not to hand them over to avoid having to pay a ransom to get them back. They also advise that motorists should politely but firmly decline any request to get into police or military vehicles.

Busy intersections in affluent residential districts and in popular tourist areas such as the *Zona Rosa* (ZOH-nah ROH-sah), literally "Pink Zone" but referring to a city's primary shopping and entertainment centers, have long been prime *mordida* locations for the police. Insiders say these locations may still be "bought and sold" like prime business real estate.

Dignidad
The Importance of "Face"

For many generations the only things most Mexicans had any control over was their pride and dignity. To compensate for their slave-like social and political status and their abject poverty, they developed an extraordinary sense of pride that was usually exercised with quiet *dignidad* (deeg-nee-DAHD) or "dignity."

But like all people who are downtrodden and oppressed by autocratic political and religious regimes, the Mexicans had a breaking point. When that point was breached they exploded in unbelievable violence. The massacre of several hundred students by government forces in Mexico City's Tlatelolco Square 1968 was one of the more conspicuous examples of the kind of official violence that had traditionally plagued the country.

By the 1970s economic and political conditions in Mexico had improved to the point that outbreaks of mass frenzy were rare, but individuals, especially macho-minded men, still reacted with violence if their pride or *dignidad* was offended.

Present-day Mexicans still have an extraordinary sense of pride and dignity, but the average person is not likely to resort to violence to avenge any indignity. There are exceptions to this, however, especially if the people involved have been drinking or if the situation involves a sexual conflict of some kind.

"Face" and *machismo* are often the same thing in the behavior of Mexican men. Any challenge to a man's masculinity, regardless of the nature of the challenge, is generally taken seriously and results in some kind of reaction.

Foreign businessmen and other visitors to Mexico need to be especially aware of not besmirching the "face" of their contacts or colleagues by unwarranted, insensitive or untimely criticisms, by ignoring them, by acting arrogant, or by failing to demonstrate an acceptable level of respect for Mexico, Mexicans, and anything they hold dear—from motherhood to revolutionary art.

The amount of "face" self-perceived by Mexicans and how protective they are of it is determined by a number of factors— their social class, age, sex, accomplishments, and so on. Even the lowest factory and farm workers expect to be treated with careful, high-toned respect, and if they don't get it they will somehow, sometime, have their revenge.

A respectful manner is especially important when dealing with people in authority, particularly government bureaucrats and law enforcement personnel.* As is invariably the case in traditionally hierarchical societies with autocratic governments, those in power positions tend to abuse their power.

---

*One of my manuscript readers took umbrage at this general statement. He said: "Yes and no! If policemen feel you are scared or intimidated they will extort you. If you are in the wrong, negotiate a payment. Minor traffic violations can usually be taken care of for less than the cost of a good meal and a few drinks. A major accident with injuries or damage to anything owned by the city (street lights, trees, etc.) will cost you dearly. However, if you are not at fault and can defend yourself in Spanish and you're in a busy area where the police don't want to create a scene, stand up for your rights. The police expect it and will respect you. Also, Mexicans will come to your aid and help defend you. Mexicans treat police with disrespect. Nothing any foreigner can say will be new to them."

Present-day efforts to introduce democratic principles and selfless behavior into government in Mexico are having a discernible effect in many areas, but it will take generations for the effects of hundreds of years of authoritarian conditioning to dissipate.

Respeto
The Importance of Respect

To most people, dignity is an internalized thing that can be maintained in the face of any kind or degree of humiliating or insulting behavior. In this sense, dignity is more of a private perspective of oneself that is not based on and does not require respect from others.

In Mexico, on the other hand, dignity and *respeto* (ray-SPAY-toh) or "respect" go hand-in-hand, and both are very public. Mexicans feel very strongly that they cannot maintain their dignity without specific, positive respect from others, and it is something that they expect and demand. ("Although in many cases they are not willing to reciprocate"—Dirk Weisheit.)

Much of the personal violence, both overt and covert, that occurs in Mexico is a direct response to a perceived lack of respect, sometimes over things that would be regarded as of no importance in the U.S. and other self-directed societies.

Respeto is especially important in male-female relations in Mexico, where it is often carried to what others consider an extreme. Macho men, for example, may accuse women who refuse to have sex with them as failing to respect their masculinity and therefore deserving of punishment.

Women believe that lovers and husbands who fail to respect them do not deserve their loyalty or sexual fidelity and therefore deserve to be cuckolded.

However, in the male-oriented world of Mexico, a husband's respect for his wife does not preclude him from having outside affairs as long as he is discreet about it (such as not bringing women into his home or associating with them in public where his wife or her friends might see them).

A great deal of the friction that occurs between Mexicans and Americans has to do with respect. Common American behavior often appears to be very disrespectful to Mexicans. This includes the casual way Americans typically dress and behave in situations that Mexicans consider formal, and the American habit of not using respect language to their elders and seniors.

There is also a lingering feeling among the majority of Mexicans—based on painful historical experience—that Americans do not respect them as a nation, as a race, or as individuals. This alone is enough to make many Mexicans especially sensitive toward any sign, real or imagined, of disrespect by American visitors or business-people.

Racial superiority exhibited toward Mexican-Americans by Anglo Americans—something which continues to this day—rankles Mexicans as well as Hispanic Americans, and can be a handicap that foreign business-people have to overcome in their dealings with Mexicans.

On a positive note, Americans in Mexico for whatever purpose generally have an advantage over upper class Mexicans and foreigners from other class-conscious countries because they are *not* class-conscious. Most Americans treat everyone on all levels of society with a fairly high level of courtesy and respect—so much so, in fact, that they are sometimes criticized for "spoiling" local people.

Americans who live in Mexico almost always endear themselves to maids and other lower-echelon employees simply by treating them with respect.

Cortesia
Living in Virtual Reality

Mexico, like all societies in which maintaining a high level of "face" is a primary factor in human relationships, has a finely detailed and institutionalized form of etiquette that makes it possible for people to live in harmony with each other as long as they follow the rules.

Mexican etiquette can be traced back to the medieval Catholic Church in Rome and the Catholicized Spanish Court in Madrid, where a highly stylized manner was equated with religious piety, fealty, "good" family, education and so on.

The Spanish *conquistadores*, colonial administrators and Catholic missionaries who poured into Mexico in the early 1500s brought the manners of the Catholic Church and high Spanish society with them.

These "Old World" manners and all the other distinctive aspects of Mexican culture that evolved during the 300-year Spanish era (1521-1821) persisted and remained virtually unchanged over these centuries be-cause the colonial administrators kept the country sealed off from the rest of the world and virtually frozen in time.

One of the most important aspects of Mexico's ritualized etiquette that has survived into modern times is the role of *cortesia* (cohr-tay-SEE-ah) or "courtesy" in interpersonal relationships.

Mexican courtesy is primarily based on demeanor and the use of respect language, including professional and honorific titles. Respect language consists of special words as well as the manner of expression, and goes well beyond just being polite.

As in all hierarchical, authoritarian societies it is essential for people to know their rank in relation to that of others so they will know how to behave toward each other. Unknowingly treating a superior as an equal or as an inferior can have disastrous results. This makes it crucial for Mexicans to be exceedingly polite with each other until they find out their relative status, after which the participants quickly assume the behavior that is appropriate for their relationship.

Mexican courtesy begins with a level of formality and politeness that has long since disappeared in many other countries. Most people greet each other formally at every encounter. Middle and upper class people, both men and women, customarily embrace each other (the famous *abrazo* / ah-BRAH-zoh)) if they have been separated for any length of time.

Since the *abrazo* is a Latin custom, generally foreigners should not initiate the embrace. When a Mexican takes the initiative it is an important sign that he has accepted the foreigner as a valued friend. An even stronger sign is when a Mexican coins a friendly nickname for the visiting businessperson.

Señor and *señorita* are used much more often in Mexico than Mr. and Mrs. are in the U.S. and some other English speaking countries. One also hears *El Señor* (Ehl say-NYOHR) as a title. It this case it means something like "The Main Man," or "His Lordship." If the marital status of a youngish looking woman is unknown it is common to refer to her as *señorita*. She will correct you if she is married.

Probably the most common honorific titles used in Mexico to show respect to people are *Don* (Dohn), *Dona* (DOH-nyah), *Maestro* (MYstroh), *Licenciado* (Lee-cen-cee-AH-doh), *Mageniero* (Mah-hay-nee-EH-roh) and *Arquitecto* (Ahr-kee-TECK-toh)—with the latter terms being more a sign of respect for the education of the individual.

Don, male, and *Dona*, female, are used only with first names, not last names: Don Miguel; Dona Maria. They are usually used to older, senior people, as a sign of respect for their age and life-time of experience, even though they might not have accomplished anything noteworthy. These terms are used when addressing some-one directly as well as in writing.

Maestro basically means "master" or "teacher" and is used when addressing people who are skilled in any art or kind of work (if they don't have a formal or professional title).

Carpenters, electricians, plumbers, etc., are routinely addressed as *maestro*, or *jefe* (HAY-fay), which has a friendlier connotation. There is often an element of flattery in the use of *maestro*, but it doesn't hurt and is good human relations. The title, along with *profesor* (pro-fay-SOHR), is especially common in Mexico City.

Academics who teach are *profesor* or *profesora* (pro-fay-SOHR-rah), and, of course, doctors are *doctor* (doc-TOHR) or *doctora* (doc-TOHR-rah). Attorneys are addressed as *licenciado*, as are other people who have university degrees but not specific professional titles. Another title that has come into its own since the development of the electronics industry in Mexico is *injenero* (en-hay-NAY-roh) or "engineer."

People in other professions as well as government agents and officials are typically addressed by their titles. Generally, only close friends use each others' first names. Foreigners should therefore be wary of addressing new acquaintances by their first names until they are asked to do so—or until their new friends began using their first name; something that is becoming more and more common among the international set in Mexico.

In any event, Americans and other foreigners doing business in Mexico—and with Mexicans outside of Mexico—do not have to be obsessed with precisely following Mexican-style courtesy.

As a general rule, Americans and others dealing with Mexicans, on whatever level, can and will get by fine by following the standards of polite, courteous behavior that is expected in genteel society in their own countries.

Excessively loud laughter in public places, an aggressive attitude, instant familiarity such as using an older or senior person's first name after being introduced, and other arrogant manners traditionally associated with Americans abroad is bad behavior in any society, including the U.S., and is more typical of unsophisticated tourists than business people.

This does not mean, of course, that foreigners who are familiar with Mexican style etiquette should not use it. There *are* advantages in "acting like a Mexican when you are in Mexico." For one thing, foreigners who know Mexican etiquette and are comfortable using it can develop the necessary personal rapport with their Mexican contacts faster and more efficiently.

But experienced Mexican businesspeople are not going to think less of foreigners who do not know or follow Mexican etiquette, or refuse to do business with them, as long as the foreigners are trustworthy, sincere, considerate enough to be genuinely responsive to the needs, expectations and concerns of their Mexican counterparts, and intelligent or sophisticated enough to treat them politely.

There are also enormous personal advantages to knowing and following Mexican etiquette when you are in Mexico. The satisfaction and pleasure that comes with being able to participate in all of the cultural nuances of life in Mexico is remarkable, and by itself is worth the effort necessary to learn how to act like a Mexican in the pursuit of these pleasures.

Just learning how to say "no" in the various Mexican Ways takes away a great many of the minor—and some of the major—aspects of Mexican life that foreigners find irritating.

A good example of this is being able to stop or reduce pestering by street vendors and touts simply by holding up an index finger and waving it slowly from side to side—a courteous enough way of saying "no" that is institutionalized in Mexican culture. [In addition to clearly signifying "no" it also signals to the vendors that you are not a naive newcomer.]

Jack Scott (Key International) recommends that foreigners in Mexico for business or pleasure should at least learn a few of the most common courtesies, such as *con permiso* (kohn payr-ME-soh) or "with your permission," used when going around or in front of a person and when leaving a room; and *una pregunta por favor* (oo-nah prey-GUUN-tah pohr fah-VOHR), figuratively, "may I ask a question?"

Another matter of courtesy that Scott suggests is that Americans should keep in mind is that in the broadest sense Mexicans also regard themselves as "Americans" and may resent the implication in the stock phrase "I'm an American." The courteous response when Americans are asked their nationality is *Yo soy Norte Americano* (yoh soy NOHR-tay Ah-may-ree-KAH-noh), "I'm North American."

One of the advantages that Mexicans have because of the importance of respect language in Mexico is that it contributes to their ability to speak their language with exceptional skill; not only in ordinary conversation but also as public speakers.

But while formal communication in Mexico is epitomized by a stylized level of courtesy that is a hallmark of Mexican etiquette, there is a flip-side that is typical of the contradictions in vertically structured authoritarian societies. (See **Obscenities and Vulgarities**.)

Some Mexicans, like their Asian counterparts, use their highly stylized *cortesia* (cohr-tay-SEE-ah) as a technique, or weapon, if you will, to gain advantages over foreigners from countries with less formal and less potent manners. In fact, some critics of Mexican behavior have likened their courtesy to the Great Wall of China, which was built to keep barbarians at bay.

Critica
Taboos against Criticism

Another key facet in the traditional character of Mexicans has been a compulsive rejection of criticism—a factor that has had a profound influence on every aspect of Mexican life, from the most mundane personal relationships to the country's political and economic systems.

Octavio Paz, one of Mexico's most famous philosopher-critics, says that virtually all of Mexico's problems—social, political and economic—from the beginning of the Spanish colonial period in 1521 down to the present, are a result of the Mexican rejection of criticism.

Paz substantiates his thesis with the obvious point that change is virtually impossible without criticism, and that Mexico's problems over the centuries have not been resolved because the culture did not allow formal, official criticism of people or institutions, thereby precluding change for the better.

Paz asserts that the Mexican abhorrence of criticism was created by the Catholic Church when, in the 16th century, it totally rejected the Reformation that resulted in the separation of the Protestant churches from the Roman Catholic Church—a movement designed to eliminate the tyrannical control that the Catholic Church exercised over both people and governments.

The primary method used by the Catholic Church to counter the Protestant-led reforms was to make any kind of criticism of the Church absolutely taboo and any deviation from the teaching of the Church punishable by torture and burning to death.

Because the tenets and rituals of the Catholic Church totally permeated the lives of Mexicans, the taboos against criticizing anybody or anything gradually pervaded the whole culture, becoming an integral part of the respect demanded by individuals, particularly those in positions of authority, as part of the personification of their dignity.

In Paz's thesis, the evils and inadequacies traditionally manifested by Mexico's political and economic systems were frozen in place for generation after generation be-cause of the cultural sanctions against criticism. In his view, Mexico did not undergo the philosophical Enlightenment that preceded the Industrial Age and redefined the way people related to religion and politics.

Taboos against directly criticizing ordinary people— particularly one's own employees—are still in force in Mexico, and foreigners doing business in the country must be wary of breaking these taboos even when criticism is warranted. In all cases, any criticizing, no matter how diplomatic or constructive, should be done in private. If the circumstances are especially sensitive it may be advisable for foreigners to use third parties to avoid causing anyone to lose face. In private situations as well, especially when drinking, sexual relationships and other types of personal confrontations are involved, direct criticism is generally regarded as insulting, and frequently results in violence of some kind.

Where public figures and public institutions are concerned, however, the taboos against criticism began losing their force in the 1960s and were virtually gone by the 1990s. Now, politicians, bureaucrats and business-people alike are regularly lampooned by their opponents, competitors and critics at large.

But, adds business consultant Ronald C. Walker, "The exercise of *constructive* criticism is still in the early stages of development in Mexico, as is constructive reform in response to valid criticism."

Foreign businesspeople should be cautious about joining in this growing chorus of public criticism because it is primarily seen as a Mexican thing.

Obviously, change in Mexico will continue to be hampered until criticism in general, and especially self-criticism by those in authority and by the elite, has become a positive facet of the culture.

Responsibilidad
Avoiding Responsibility

One cultural characteristic of new untrained Mexican employees that expatriate managers of foreign firms in Mexico find especially frustrating is their inexperience with, and reluctance to assume, personal responsibility, particularly when it comes to acting on their own initiative to make sure that work gets done.

There is good reason for this still common Mexican behavior. Generally speaking, throughout Mexican history hired hands in any capacity were not allowed to act on their own. Such behavior was totally unacceptable and there were strong sanctions against it.

Mexican bosses did not delegate authority, and insisted on making all decisions. Any attempt by a sub-ordinate to assume even the smallest amount of the boss's authority was regarded as an underhanded act, if not outright treachery, and was dealt with accordingly.

For most of the 300-year Spanish reign in Mexico this cultural conditioning had both racial and class overtones. Indians were treated as being unable to reason and therefore incapable of properly handling personal responsibility. The later Mestizos were so distrusted and despised that allowing them to make decisions on their own was unthinkable to the Spanish overlords.

By the time Mexico gained its independence from Spain in 1821 this syndrome was so deeply embedded in the society that it had become an essential part of the culture.

Freedom from Spain did not change the economic, social or political situation for the overwhelming majority of Mexicans. They remained poverty-stricken, politically powerless, at the bottom of society, and subject to the kind of authoritarian rule that made it impossible for ordinary employees to assume any kind of responsibility.

Present-day society in Mexico is still primarily authoritarian. In medium-sized and smaller firms, most bosses still do not delegate authority. Most employees naturally leave all decision-making up to their bosses, and expect to receive precise instructions from their superiors. In smaller operations this syndrome is one of the many cultural factors that foreign employers in Mexico must deal with. Most new employees, unless they were educated abroad, still have to be culturally reprogrammed before they are able to take the initiative in making decisions and doing things on their own.

The situation is changing rapidly in the larger firms, however. Says one veteran expatriate manager: "Major multi-nationals demand aggressive managers. Many Mexicans can hold their own with any foreign manager."

When things go wrong in Mexico there is still a strong tendency for those in positions of authority to try to shift the blame to their subordinates or to outside influences—which, of course, is common enough everywhere.

La Verdad
Mexican-Style Truth

Historically the people of Mexico have not been protected by justly enforced laws, and have been subject to the passions and selfish interests of those in power. (Mexicans are fond of saying that in Mexico laws are like rubber; forever being stretched to benefit those in charge of enforcing them.)

Over the centuries, the only way Mexicans could survive, regardless of their social class or their position, was to please others one way or the other. This meant that they had to interpret each situation from two personal viewpoints—the other party's and their own.

Given this arbitrary, situational nature of traditional ethics and morality in Mexico it follows automatically that *la verdad* (lah vahr-DAD) or "the truth" would be determined by the circumstances at hand rather than fundamental principles having to do with right and wrong.

As far as Mexicans were concerned, "the truth" was whatever would provide them with the most protection. As time went by, "the truth" became telling people what they wanted to hear; what would allow the speaker to maintain "face," and not disappoint or anger the other person. Eventually, social etiquette demanded that people not tell the unvarnished truth even when there was no danger in it.

Still today in Mexico *la verdad* in social and minor business matters often has little if any relationship with reality. People routinely say things and make commitments that are intended to make others feel good at that moment in time rather than actually inform them.

Personal anecdotes about life and work in Mexico are filled with examples of attitudes and behavior that often make more literal and truth-minded foreigners question the common sense of typical Mexicans.

One thing that especially frustrates foreigners in Mexico, particularly outside of the international communities of large urban areas, is the Mexican habit of not giving full answers to questions.

An example recounted by James O'Reilly and Larry Habegger in their insightful *Travelers' Tales MEXICO* (Travelers' Tales, Inc./ San Francisco) that immediately comes to mind is a "bus story."

In this case the foreign traveler asks if there is a bus to a certain town. The ticket seller at the bus station says "no."

A number of diplomatic follow-up questions eventually reveal that although there are no buses that go just *to* that town, there are several that stop there on their way through and beyond the town.

The ticket seller was not being untruthful or evasive. He was just giving the shortest, simplest answer possible, and did not feel obligated to volunteer any additional information—a kind of behavior that naturally mystifies and frustrates people who are not familiar with the Mexican Way.

This particular mindset, which is also common in the Orient, is an unconscious attempt to stay uninvolved and avoid exposing oneself to the kind of dangers that are built into traditionally authoritarian societies that deny most basic human rights to ordinary people.

Those who have had experience with this kind of traditional behavior know that it is often necessary to act like an attorney interrogating a passive, reluctant witness to get the "whole story" out of someone.

Mexicans who are better educated and have been exposed to a less emotional approach to life are gradually overcoming these automatic protective ploys. But such behavior will no doubt continue to be a significant part of the character of most Mexicans for some time.

There is also a flip-side to the psychological conditioning of how Mexicans respond to questions. When they do not know the answer to a question there is a culturally conditioned impulse to make up an answer to avoid disappointing the questioner or appearing impolite or uninformed—another response that is right out of Asia.

On higher social and economic levels, however, this situation is changing. Many Mexicans who are involved in international business and international affairs in general, particularly those with experience abroad, have switched from personal or policy-oriented truth to principle-oriented truth.

Still, foreign businesspeople operating in Mexico must keep their cultural antennae up at all times to identify the kind of truth they are being told, especially where small routine things are concerned.

In referring to the existence of "multiple truths" in Mexico, Ronald C. Walker notes that accurate business-related information is one of the rarest commodities in Mexico because typically there are two or more different answers or sets of information to the same question.

Walker adds: "This makes it extremely difficult for Mexican businesspeople themselves to obtain accurate, current information, and, of course, it has a tendency to drive foreign businesspeople up the wall.

"For example, government figures on financial reserves, or unemployment, etc., can be completely unrealistic and official at the same time. The office of the public register of property can have several maps of a city limits on file that are all different and all completely legal. A Mexican businessman may support a certain position in a meeting for hours, with good arguments, and then taken a completely opposite position without any explanation whatsoever."

Imagen
The Mexican Self-Image

One of the traditional American images of Mexicans was that they did not try to improve their living standard because they were lazy and simply not interested in helping themselves. That image was patently false.

Unemployment has been high in Mexico since the days of the Spanish colonial period. Historically in some villages, towns and cities, as many as 40 to 50 percent of the adult population was unemployed or underemployed (a situation that continues to be the case even today, notes consultant Ronald C. Walker).

In addition, malnutrition and stomach ailments were also endemic among the poor in Mexico, sapping the energy and ambition of millions of people, and often preventing them from taking full advantage of any educational opportunities they had. Large numbers of these poverty-stricken and often ill people lived in make-shift lean-to's or huts, or were altogether home-less. Their presence on the streets of Mexico gave the impression to those who didn't know any better that Mexicans were congenitally lazy.

Some of this foreign image of Mexico lingers on, in part kept alive by differences in cultural outlook. Americans have been religiously oriented to regard not working as immoral. Mexicans were traditionally conditioned to believe that "living" came first and working came second in the overall scheme of things.

But in Mexico City, Guadalajara, Monterrey and other major industrial areas, this cultural difference is rapidly disappearing. Most Mexican businessmen put in as many long, hard hours as their foreign counterparts.

Says Michael T. Eakins: "My experience in the retail food industry is that our Mexican counterparts work just as hard and as many hours as we do. While it is true that they honor the traditional two-to-three hour afternoon *la comida* (lah coh-ME-dah) break, they can also be found in their offices until 7 p.m. or later, and they always work on Saturdays."

In fact, a growing number of Mexicans in the middle and upper classes are deliberately adopting the American work-ethic—not because they think it is better than the Mexican ethic, but because they believe it is the only way they can become competitive and keep their country from being swallowed up by the U.S. and other aggressive nations.

Foreigners should keep in mind that the *imagen* (ee-MAH-hane) or image that Mexicans have of themselves is that they are a highly cultured, sophisticated, proud and talented people whose personal morals are superior, whose family system is exemplary, and who know more about how to live a spiritually, emotionally and intellectually satisfying life than most people.

Foreigners may not agree with this self-portrait of Mexicans, but if they want to get along with Mexicans and succeed in doing business with them, they must respect their image of themselves.

At the same time that a strong, positive self-image is a vital part of the psychological profile of Mexicans, there are cultural taboos prohibiting them from trying to make themselves look good by claiming qualifications they do not have, and calling for a modest, humble approach when talking about themselves.

The few people who break these taboos by exaggerating their experiences and abilities are often referred to as *mitoteros* (me-toh-TAY-rohs), which might be loosely translated as "story tellers." Other people generally delight in exposing *mitoteros* as frauds.

Another aspect of the self-image of Mexicans may be a bit surprising. Despite the cultural programming of Mexicans in precise, highly homogeneous role-playing, they do not like to be thought of or treated en masse as the similarly programmed Japanese do. Just like Americans and other individualistic nationalities, Mexicans think of themselves as totally separate entities and expect to be treated as such. They also do not like to be ignored.

Regardless of their social level or circumstances they expect to be treated with courtesy and respect by everyone. The gate man at the villa of some well-to-do family or at a factory compound expects to be acknowledged daily with a friendly wave or comment by his ultimate boss.

Foreign businesspeople visiting factories in Mexico should make a point of greeting and chatting briefly with foremen and bench workers. It is also important to get to know the secretaries and clerks in offices, learning something about their families and their special interests.

Executive secretaries are particularly proud of their positions and possessive of their power. Like their U.S. counterparts, they practically control who gets to see the boss, and when.

Foreign businesspeople making frequent calls on the same offices should always take gifts or novelties for the secretaries. Such things as unusual letter openers, four-color ball point pens, or small toys for their children are always welcome, as are chocolates.

Key International's Jack Scott said this kind of personal touch was a key factor in his success in Mexico. "I always sent faxes to the individuals I wanted to visit, suggesting a date and time for my appointments. Since these messages went through the secretaries, I almost always got the appointments I wanted."

Scott related another example of how good relations with a secretary worked to his advantage. "When visiting the electronics division of one of the largest industrial complexes in Mexico—a multi-million dollar a year customer—I always liked to meet and talk to the director and general manager even though my primary business was with the purchasing officers.

"I made it a point to call on the director's secretary to let her know I was in the building and while there would like to visit briefly with Engineer Tamayo, the director. You can image how well the orders went when Director Tamayo's secretary came into the purchasing manager's office and informed me that Director Tamayo would like to see me when I finished, and if I was free he would like for me to join him in the executive dining room for lunch. She enjoyed the 'game' as much as I did."

Scott added: "An additional point is, in Mexico work from the top down. Don't waste time climbing up."

Lealtad
The Human Equation

Employee turn-over in most foreign-owned Mexican firms has consistently been higher than the national average, bringing into question the *lealtad* (lay-ahl-TAHD) or "loyalty" of Mexican managers and workers.

Generally speaking, Mexican loyalty is not based on such abstract things as principles and promises, or any feelings of guilt associated with these things. The loyalty of Mexicans is much more likely to be measured in terms of the quality of the human relations involved in any employment situation.

Managers and workers who do not believe that the management philosophy and practices of the company they work for are sufficiently "human oriented" to meet their standards do not feel any special obligation to be loyal to that company. At the same time, employees who are unhappy with the human relations policies and practices of a company will almost never do their best for the company, and are generally uncooperative and passive in their overall attitude and manner as well.

Employers must therefore first address the human relations issues in order to create and maintain employee loyalty and diligence. This involves such things as taking a genuine interest in the personal affairs of their workers, making employees feel welcome and appreciated in the factory and office, and respecting their self-image, especially their sense of dignity.

Of course, salary and other benefits are important factors in company loyalty in Mexico, but the more personally oriented and family-like a company, the more loyal its employees are apt to be. Managers, however, are likely to go where the money is. In the late 1980s and early 1990s, it became fairly common for managers to jump from one company to another, sometimes doubling their salaries.

Whatever the situation, loyalty in Mexico is almost al-ways expressed in personal terms—to individual bosses—rather than to corporate (or government) entities, making it vital that managers be good "people" persons.

Personal secretaries in Mexico are especially loyal to their superiors, and constitute a factor that foreign busi-nesspeople must take into consideration to do business effectively, says Michael Eakins. "Like many of their counterparts in the United States, secretaries in Mexico see themselves as guardians of the executive office gates. Having a friendly working relationship with them is an important key to doing business there," Eakins added.

Foreign companies evaluating managers for assignment to Mexico would be wise to rank personality, people skills and cross-cultural sensitivity on the same level, if not higher, as technical skills and knowledge of the company, its products, and policies.

Simpatico
The Sympathy Syndrome

In my book, *Mexico's Business & Cultural Code Words**, I ranked *simpatico* (seem-PAH-tee-coh) as one of the top five words in the Mexican language because of the importance of the role it plays in Mexican life. The literal English meaning of *simpatico* is, of course, sympathetic, but in its Mexican context *simpatico* goes well beyond the idea of being sympathetic toward a person or a cause. Its meaning is far more comprehensive.

---

*This book is also available in a trade paperback edition under the name, *There's a Word for It in Mexico!*

In addition to incorporating the concept of a sympathetic nature, *simpatico* also infers that a person is loyal, trustworthy and supportive, and can be counted on in times of trouble to do everything possible to help family and friends. *Simpatico* implies understanding as well as agreement—something that can be both misleading and dangerous to the outsider who does not know the full cultural nuances of the word.

In Anglo cultures, a person may sympathize with somebody or some cause but oppose them on principle or for some other reason. In Mexico the *simpatico* person is generally expected to be an ally regardless of the circum-stances.

One of the standards by which Mexicans measure foreigners is how they score on the *simpatico* scale. They are very unlikely to develop the personal bonds that are necessary for them to go into a business relationship with someone whose *simpatico* score is not within an acceptable margin.

Walter J. Gomez notes, however, that to younger generations of Mexicans the cultural implications of *simpatico* are not always as deep or as comprehensive as in the past. "As far as many young people today are concerned, a *simpatico* person is just someone who is fun to be around; someone you like," he said.

Buena Gente
One of the Good Guys

The phrase *buena gente* (BWAY-nah HAYNE-tay), or "good person," might be described as the constant companion of *simpatico*. In its Mexican usage, it is hard to imagine a *buena gente* who is not also *simpatico*.

As usual, the cultural meaning of *buena gente* goes well beyond the common, colloquial English translation. The phrase still retains all of the original meaning and flavor of the word "good" in the biblical and philosophical sense. A person described as *buena gente* is someone who is kind, considerate, well-mannered, educated, sincere, loyal, trustworthy, dependable, and can be counted on to behave according to the highest Mexican standards.

The cultural antennae of Mexicans are always up and always receiving input on the *buena gente* qualities of everyone they encounter. And again, if a person does not measure up to their standards any relationship is likely to be at arm's length and breakable at any time.

Foreign businesspeople wanting to succeed in Mexico must first prove that they qualify as *buena gente*—something that Dirk Weisheit says is far more difficult than it sounds.

Machismo
The Masculinity Cult

Understanding and functioning effectively in Mexican society, in both business and private affairs, requires an in-depth knowledge of factors affecting male-male and male-female relationships, and considerable skill in conducting oneself in a culturally correct manner.

One of the key cultural factors that sets the style and tone for virtually all relationships in Mexico is subsumed in the term *machismo* (mah-CHEES-moh), which is generally translated into English as a "masculinity cult" as a way of emphasizing the importance of its role in Mexican life. The concept and practice of male machoism has, of course, been around for a long time and is well-known. The point here is that the traditional *machismo* of Mexico went well beyond the form that was common in most other countries of the world.

Mexico's exaggerated *machismo* was a mutation resulting from the fusion of attitudes and practices that developed among the Berber-Arab Moors who brought them to Spain when they invaded and occupied that country in the 8th century, and similar attitudes and behavior that were typical of the Aztecs and a number of other Mexican Indians when the Spanish *conquistadores* arrived in Mexico in 1519.

The Moors and most Mexican Indians regarded men as inherently superior to women, spiritually, intellectually and otherwise. They also believed that women had to be kept submissive and obedient by force, a belief that obviously derived in part at least from the primitive stud complex that is commonly seen in lower animals. (This suggests that men, like their animal relatives, were originally genetically programmed to have multiple "wives" or keep harems.)

In any event, the combination of Moorish machoism and the male superiority complex of Spanish Catholicism was already a heady brew by the time it reached Mexico in 1519. When the Indian contribution was added over the next several generations it became even more volatile.

The ingredient that was to complete the masculine mindset and give it its peculiar Mexican form was contributed by Spanish-Indian Mestizos—the offspring of Spanish men and Indian women. As virtual outcasts for the first several generations of their existence, the Mestizos seethed with anger and frustration at their poverty, powerlessness and outcast status.

In an effort to compensate for their degradation, urban Mestizos men took the concept and practice of machoism to an extreme, making it the basis for virtually everything they said and did.

Mexican sociologists say that another aspect of this hyper machoism by Mestizos was a defense reaction resulting from the fact that throughout the 300-year Spanish colonial period

Spanish men had virtually unrestrained sexual access to both Indian women and Mestizo women.

According to these sociologists, Mestizo men became convinced that all women were literally conditioned to be unfaithful, and that the only way they could compete with the Spaniards was to emphasize their own masculinity to an extraordinary degree.

This extreme form of *machismo* played a key role in the violence that was to plague Mexican society during the 1800s and the first decades of the 1900s, particularly the mass and often senseless killings that occurred during the war for independence from Spain in 1810-21 and the revolutionary war of 1910-21.

Macho-induced violence among the general population in Mexico had subsided dramatically by the 1960s and 70s, but it has continued to persist in its most violent form among the criminal element and in law enforcement agencies.

Machismo remains a key element in all personal relationships on all levels of society in present-day Mexico, but the once fearful scourge has lost most of its virulence, particularly among the middle and upper classes, and is now viewed—at least by men—as one of the most admirable facets of Mexican culture; responsible for the strong family ties and the high level of etiquette that is characteristic of Mexican behavior.

Generally speaking, *machismo* requires Mexican men to put on a fearless air, to flaunt their masculinity, to be conspicuously passionate in their relations with women, to be sexually aggressive, to drink, to be strict with their wives and children, and to take revenge when they are wronged.

It is very important for foreigners dealing with Mexico to be aware of both the nature and ongoing role of *machismo* because it continues to be a key factor in how Mexicans perceive themselves, how they behave, and how they respond to others in both personal and business situations.

Foreigners who attempt to match the macho behavior of their Mexican friends or counterparts—and some do—often get themselves into trouble because they are not prepared for the consequences.

Mucha Mujer
The Femininity Cult

One of the many contradictions in Mexican culture that was created by Roman Catholicism was the traditional attitude that all women were real live manifestations of the Virgin Mary—that they maintained, or should maintain, their "virginal" state even after marriage, and were therefore totally different from men.

This virgin mother complex, created and sustained by men—not women, of course—influenced virtually every aspect of traditional Mexican culture, from the chaperon-based courting system, the ritual of worshipping motherhood, the practice of mistress-keeping, the widespread practice of prostitution, to the crudest and most insulting language.

In this Church-inspired syndrome, all of the evils of Mexico came to be linked with the sexual violation of the Virgin Mother, and all that was good was attributed to her love, her forbearance and her forgiveness.

An unholy alliance between the male-dominated Church and men at large laid the burden of sustaining the Virgin Mother syndrome on women—and in response to a gonad-driven ego that directed their lives, Church leaders and men conspired to make this burden as all-encompassing and as restrictive as possible.

Santas
Women as Saints

The Catholic Church of Mexico and men in general sought to achieve their goals of keeping women servile in a number of ways that had been perfected by male-dominated societies ages ago. In addition to the threat and use of force, Mexican men put women on pedestals and showered them with compliments for their virginity before marriage and a virginal life of service and sacrifice afterward.

Mexico's male-dominated Church established rules that made it taboo for women to think or behave in an independent manner, particularly in exercising their sexuality; and they conditioned women to believe that sacrificing themselves to the Church and to men was the only path to salvation.

In this masculine dominated environment every woman was expected to see herself as a candidate for sainthood and to behave accordingly, regardless of the circumstances or temptations. But this was not all the burden that the Church and men put on women.

Serpientes
Women as Serpents

The Church also preached that women were inherently evil. While praising and glorifying them on one hand, it constantly reminded them that they were like serpents in the Garden of Eden, that they could not be trusted and that men had a right to "protect" them from their sexual proclivities and to punish them for their transgressions.

Women were praised and honored for their femininity and damned for their sexuality. This two-faced male attitude was designed to accomplish two things: to satisfy the programmed hyper virility of men, and to make it possible for men to control sexual access to women in general but especially to their wives, daughters and sweethearts.

Mexican women were thus trapped in a double-bind. Primed in sexuality from an early age, they were then prevented from expressing their sexuality except under carefully defined and controlled circumstances.

Women who deviated in the slightest from this minutely programmed form of behavior were condemned and punished, first by their fathers and brothers, and then by boy friends and husbands. Total banishment from the family was commonplace.

The female equivalent of the *macho* man was a *mala mujer* (MAH-lah muu-HEHR) or "bad woman," meaning a woman who thought for herself and aggressively pursued her own goals.

This environment resulted in Mexican women typically developing several personalities—the demure virgin girl, the blatant temptress, the devoted mother, the pious church-goer, and the clever manipulator cunning enough to control lovers and husbands.

But no matter how much skill Mexican women developed in their efforts to survive in the male-dominated society they were still treated as inferior and were primarily used by men as instruments of utility and selfish pleasure.*

---

*Machismo, particularly its "protect women" syndrome, is said to be stronger in Brazil and other Latin American countries than in Mexico. An American businessman related this old tale.

During the Perez Gemini regime he went to Caracas, Venezuela with the factory service engineer for Roots Motors and the Rover Company of England. The engineer had relatives in Caracas, and one evening took a female cousin out for dinner. Following dinner, he escorted the lady to her front door where he gave her a cousinly goodbye kiss on the cheek.

This public "sexual display" was seen by a member of the *Guardia Nacional*. The guard arrested the engineer. When the American businessman discovered the next morning that the engineer had not returned to their hotel, he had a Venezuela business associate contact the local jails.

Learning that the engineer was, in fact, in jail, and the reason why, the American called the lady's brothers and asked their help in getting the engineer released. They refused his request for help because to admit that their sister had been kissed in public would compromise the reputation of their sister as well as the rest of the family.

The American then enlisted the aid of his representative firm's lawyer. It took the lawyer two days to get the engineer out of jail.

Emancipacion
More Freedom for Women

It was not until the second half of the 20th century that economic, political and social evolution in Mexico began gradually freeing women from absolute male domination, allowing them the right to education, and to have some freedom of choice.

By the end of the 20th century Mexican society had evolved to the point that women were just beginning to play a significant role beyond the scope of wives and mothers, participating in the economy outside of their homes, and playing a limited role in politics.

This gradual evolution will inevitably continue, but there is virtually no possibility that Mexican women will be fully emancipated in the American sense in the foreseeable future. The concept that men and women are different and that there is a man's world and a woman's world is too deeply ingrained in the Mexican psyche for equality to become the norm any time soon.

In fact, the concept of the proper role of the sexes accounts for one of the biggest gaps between Mexican and American cultures. Mexicans see the movement in the United States toward full male-female equality in all things as a major factor in the collapse of the American family and violence in American society.

Foreign businessmen and businesswomen visiting and working in Mexico must be aware of this cultural difference and take it into consideration in all of their dealings. Among other things, the male American practice of treating working women like "one of the boys" doesn't work at all in Mexico.

The impact of male-female role-playing in Mexico is everywhere, from how men look at women as they walk down the street or pass through a hotel lobby—and how women react to this scrutiny—to male-female relations in business settings.

Mujeres y Negocios
Women and Business

Women did not begin to appear in the Mexican world of business in any significant number until the 1970s. Prior to that, as in other male-dominated, authoritarian societies, business was a man's world in which women were generally not welcome and only a few dared enter, usually as secretaries or maids.

Young Mexican women who went to work as secretaries for foreign companies in Mexico in the 1960s were pioneers in breaking the taboos against women in business offices. Generally from affluent families, well-educated, and mostly attractive, these young women became role models for other Mexican women wanting to escape from their traditional roles as domestics, housewives and mothers.

Still today in Mexico the workplace is strewn with masculine challenges that women must contend with, whether in a factory or in an office. Generally speaking, Mexican men view women in business as females first and businesspersons second, and are not totally comfortable dealing with them.

As elsewhere in the world, women in Mexico also generally have to work harder than men to prove themselves. "Unfortunately," says one veteran male expatriate, "this creates some real bitches! I have had some bad experiences working for Mexican women. One of my female bosses had such a bad attitude that seven highly qualified male managers quit within a short period of time."

The veteran added: "Also, foreign executives wanting to hire young Mexican women should keep in mind that they will eventually marry, have kids and quit work because the family takes precedence over the company. You don't see many older Mexican women working as executives."

Also generally speaking, most Mexican men treat foreign businesswomen with courtesy and respect if the women dress and behave in a conspicuously professional manner. But they too, have to perform especially well in order to hold their own.

A veteran American businesswoman with decades of experience in Latin America listed seven qualifications that a foreign businesswoman needs to succeed in Mexico and other "macho" countries:

1) Be completely familiar with her company's products and service.
2) Have the authority to speak for and commit her company, including negotiate and sign contracts.

3) Speak Spanish well enough to understand and converse on a social and business level.

4) Be familiar with the customs and etiquette of the country.

5) *Pay for entertaining clients.*

6) Dress in a stylish but conservation fashion, and definitely stay away from pants suits.

7) Enjoying working with and associating with people from a different national and cultural background.

Working women, Mexican or foreign, who dress and behave in a sensually provocative manner are especially likely to be inundated with attention from male co-workers who have long been conditioned to take such sexual displays as an invitation to shower them with *piropos* (pee-ROH-pohs), or "sex-oriented complimentary comments," and make other advances.

However, as in Asia and elsewhere, foreign companies operating in Mexico often find that Mexican women are among their most valuable employees, not only in terms of intelligence, diligence and loyalty, but also because of their intuitive understanding of situations.

Another point that foreign businesspeople in Mexico should keep in mind is that still today Mexican businessmen generally do not discuss business with their wives, and most do not bring their wives to business receptions or include them in business-oriented functions.

Another point worthy of mention: because of their cultural conditioning, Mexican women are much more aware of the sensual aspect of their bodies and the bodies of men than is generally the case among women in Anglo cultures. They are able to turn their sensuality up at will, like a rheostat light switch, radiating a sexuality that few men can resist.

Hora Mexicana
Dealing with Polychronic People

In his book, *Beyond Culture* (Anchor Press, Garden City, New York), social scientist Edward T. Hall came up with the word "polychronic" to describe a cultural feature that is characteristic of Mexican behavior. Hall identified two kinds of time values in different cultures: one that he called "monochronic," which he defined as "one thing at a time" time; and "polychronic," or "many things at a time" time.

By this definition, Americans and most other people in Anglo-European cultures are monochronic or "M-time" people, meaning they are conditioned to concentrate on one thing at a time. While Mexicans, other Hispanics and most Asians are polychronic or "P-time" people who typically engage in many things, going from one to the other in the same time frame.

Monochronic people see time as constantly moving forward in a straight line, and compulsively measure time in tiny segments to keep track of its passing. They schedule things to happen one at a time in specific time frames, and are obsessed with things happening "on time." Any deviation in this precisely structured use of time is very upsetting to M-people.

Polychronic people, on the other hand, have a much more amorphous view of time. It is more of a seasonal thing in the sense that there is a morning, a mid-day, an evening, days and nights, and so on, but these periods are more or less open-ended. They are not precisely segmented into so many minutes and hours, and do not start or stop on the dot.

P-people routinely schedule, or allow, many things to occur at the same time, and are at ease in juggling them around so that eventually all of them—or at least some of them—get done.

This includes agreeing to more than one appointment at the same time, accepting more than one work assignment that is "supposed" to be done in the same time frame, intermittently doing two or three things during the same time period, and so on.

Mexicans have traditionally viewed time as moving in a circle; not in a straight line. Time not "used" is not lost because it comes around again. Doing things according to a precise time schedule is not that vital because they can always be done later, and so on.

Mexicans tend to see scheduling things by the minute as inhuman, as unfriendly—as behaving too much like robots or other machines—and taking the variety and spice out of life.

On the other hand, monochronic people tend to see the amorphous view and loose use of time by P-people as a cultural weakness; as a character failing that needs to be "fixed." A great deal of the time and energy of M-time people in Mexico is therefore spent coping with the way Mexicans view and use time, and, where employees are concerned, trying to convert them to M-time.

Not surprisingly, Mexicans think that monochronic people are too obsessed with time and getting things done on precise schedules and that it is the values of M-time that are irrational and wrong. The Mexican view is that "living" is more important than following mechanical schedules and getting things done in as short a time as possible.*

---

*The Mexican view and use of time is apparently more Spanish and Arabic than Mexican Indian. The early Mayan obsession with time—which resulted in them becoming the world's most accurate date-keepers—appears to have been oriented toward keeping calendars of religious and other auspicious events, past and future. But it may also have caused them to clock daily personal activities as well. Aztecs believed that time was "used up" each day, in the sense that the sun set each evening and required the blood of a human sacrifice to ensure that it would rise again the next morning, resulting in them being very sensitive to the passing of time.

Prior to industrialization all people everywhere were more or less on polychronic time, so monochronic time is relative new in the human experience. Polychronic time has survived in Mexico not only because the Hispanic temperament is different but also because industrialization was very slow in coming to the country.

P-time and industrial progress are virtually incompatible, however, so as Mexico becomes more and more mechanized and linked to the international pace of business, P-time is gradually diminishing in business situations.

Of course, it is the P-time syndrome that is responsible for the cultural ramifications of the words *ahora* (ah-OHR-rah), *ahorita* (ah-ohr-REE-tah) and *manana* (mah-NYAH-nah).

Manana is usually translated as "tomorrow" but when it is used it means more like "not now."

By the same token, notes Dirk Weisheit, "*ahorita* does not mean 'right now,' it means 'in a while.'"

In Mexico being on time for social appointments usually means arriving an hour to an hour and a half after the set time. Anything up to two hours after the set time is considered good etiquette.

"On time" for business appointments—when "American time" is not specified—takes another tack, however. Generally speaking, Mexican businessmen and government officials expect people who have appointments with them to show up on time, even if they themselves are still in the midst of another meeting or have not yet arrived at their offices.

Making people wait in this manner has been explained as being a way Mexicans demonstrate their authority and importance. Whatever the rationale, the burden is on the visitor to stay calm and polite and put up with the inconvenience. People who are familiar with this custom—and know they are going to have to wait, either from experience or because they have been told—make a practice of taking paperwork with them so they can do something worthwhile with the time. Cellular phones have made it a lot easier for people waiting for appointments to keep busy.

Other occasions when *hora Americana* (OHR-rah Ah-may-ree-CAH-nah) is the rule include important meetings with high-level business contacts, appointments for professional services (with dentists, doctors, attorneys, etc.) job interviews, school examinations, and big-city bus, train and plane departures—although arriving "on time" then having to wait is also common.

In rural Mexico most things are naturally on *hora Mexicana* (OHR-rah May-he-CAH-no), or "Mexican time." The general rule there is that things begin when everyone concerned is ready for them to begin.

One example: while many buses in Mexico depart on precise schedules, there are others that leave whenever the bus drivers or someone else decides that the bus is "full"—and being full doesn't have anything to do with how many seats there are on a bus. The buses may leave when there is no more room to squeeze anyone else in; or when the bus drivers have finished eating or talking to their friends—things that can give un-initiated time-centered people fits.

Old Mexican hand Michael Eakins has a warning for ex-perienced travelers who are accustomed to arriving at airports ten minutes before the scheduled departure times of their flights. He says that even *hora Americana* often isn't enough in Mexico because airline airport staff frequently reassign seats that haven't been personally claimed as much as 45 minutes before departure time.

Paciencia
The Virtue of Patience

There is unending pressure on Mexicans who are involved in international business to change their mind-clock over to M-time, and growing numbers, particularly those who have had considerable experience abroad, are making the switch.

But most Mexicans are not interested in changing over to M-time because they regard the disadvantages of monochronic be-havior as too much of a sacrifice, pointing out that it is de-trimental to their own health and limits the amount of time they have to spend with their families and friends, something they believe should take precedence over work.

It is unlikely that the majority of Mexicans will ever convert entirely to monochronic time, so the only way that M-time people can survive and succeed in Mexico, without eventually imploding from stress, is to reorient themselves to a consid-erable degree to Mexican time.

For most foreigners, this reorientation must begin with a crash course in *paciencia* (pah-cee-EN-cee-ah) or "patience," which includes controlling their impatience and hoping that eventually the reprogramming will transcend their original con-ditioning to the point that getting on and staying on Mexican time will no longer be a frustrating challenge but will come naturally.

The first introduction to polychronic time for many foreign businesspeople newly arrived in Mexico is the two to three-hour lunch break in the afternoon, which can seem like a sinful waste to those who have not yet been initiated into the Mexican way of doing things, and the importance of this ritualistic custom.

Generally, most foreigners do adapt fairly quickly and fairly well to the slower pace of life in Mexico. Their primary problem thereafter is dealing with their own colleagues back home who are still on monochronic time and are unable or unwilling to accept the idea that the Mexican time clock cannot be easily and quickly speeded up just by twisting a few arms.

El Nacionalismo
Pride and Prejudice

Another factor that impacts on Mexico's international business relations is their love for their country and their pride in their culture.

Unlike post-World War II generations of Americans who were indoctrinated in leftist liberalism by their college professors and who thereafter made something of a cult of criticizing the U.S., young people in Mexican schools are systematically imbued with strong feelings of nationalism and an unbounded pride in their country.

I recall one extraordinary incident that occurred on the Mexican side of the border in Nogales, Sonora that dramatically demonstrates the difference between *nacionalismo* (nah-cee-oh-EES-moh) or "nationalism" in the U.S. and Mexico.

Several American students from the University of Arizona in Tucson had just passed through the Immigration checkpoint and were walking toward the tourist shops a short distance away. One of the male students had sewn a small American flag on the seat of his trousers.

A middle-aged Mexican businessman who was a long-time resident of Nogales and well-known in Arizona as a goodwill ambassador between Sonora and Arizona, happened to be at the border crossing and saw the American flag on the student's rear-end.

The Mexican businessman shouted at the students to stop. They apparently thought he was an Immigration official and obeyed his order.

He then proceeded to lecture the young man, saying: "If you have no more respect for your country than to wear its flag on your ass, how can we expect you to respect *our* country! We do not want your kind of people here! If I ever see you again I will have you thrown in jail! Now take care of your business and leave Mexico!"

Mexicans are fully aware of the social and cultural weaknesses of the U.S. and have no qualms about voicing them in the right setting, but they regard it as extremely ill-mannered and condescending for Americans to criticize their own country in an attempt to ingratiate themselves with Mexicans.

At the same time, privately most Mexicans are also more critical of their own government and a number of their institutions than foreigners usually are, but they regard criticism from outsiders as meddling in their affairs, and they resent it.

Foreign businesspeople wanting to establish good working relationships with Mexicans will be much more likely to succeed if they emphasize the positive aspects of Mexico and their own country, and spend their time and energy trying to make things better rather than tearing them down.

September 16, Mexican Independence Day, when Mexicans celebrate their independence from Spain in 1821, and the *Cinco de Mayo* (CEEN-coh day MAH-yoh) or May 5th celebration when Mexicans celebrate their victory over the French occupation army at the Battle of Puebla in 1862, are occasions when Mexicans demonstrate their nationalism with extraordinary gusto.

On the nights of May 4th and September 15th, it is common for Mexicans to gather in small and large groups in bars, clubs, restaurants and other locations and at 11 p.m. began shouting *Viva Mexico!* (VEE-vah MEH-he-coh!).

Some turn the shouting into a marathon that continues without stopping for the full hour, ending at midnight in a frenzy of voices.

It is also the custom on the morning of September 16, for the mayors of towns and cities to stand on the steps of the *palacio municipal* (pah-LAH-cee-oh moo-nee-cee-PAHL) or "city hall" and be the first to shout the *el grito* (ehl GREE-toh), or "the cry" (for independence)—*Mexicanos! Viva Mexico!*—with which the priest Dolores Hidalgo announced the beginning of the revolutionary war against Spain in 1810.

Extranjeros
The Gringo Syndrome

Mexico's experiences with foreign countries have not been happy ones. Mexicans won their independence from Spain in 1821 after a bloody 11-year war. Within the next decade, thousands of Americans settled in the Texas portion of the sparsely populated Mexican state of Coahuila.

Starting in 1833 these American residents of Mexico began a series of rebellions against local Mexican authorities that led to Mexico losing Texas in 1836 when its predominately American inhabitants defeated General Santa Ana in a decisive battle and declared it an independent country. It was to remain an independent country only until 1845 when it was annexed by the U.S. as a state.

This action led to border clashes between U.S. and Mexican forces. In 1847 the United States declared war on Mexico and invaded the country. The American army quickly captured and occupied Mexico City, withdrawing only after Mexico agreed to give up over half of its national territory (Texas, New Mexico, Arizona, Nevada, Utah, California and part of Colorado)—for which the U.S. paid a token sum of $15 (or $18!) million. Rumor had it that most of the money went to Santa Ana personally—not to the Mexican government.

In 1862 a combined force of Spanish, French and English warships bombarded and then occupied Veracruz, ostensibly to force the Mexican government to pay some old debts. Shortly thereafter, a large French force invaded the whole of Mexico, defeated the Mexican army in a series of battles, incorporated the country into the French empire, and brought in the Archduke Maximilian of Austria to be the emperor of Mexico.

Mexicans regained their independence in 1867 after a series of bloody battles in which they finally defeated the French occupation army, captured Maximilian, and executed him.

From the 1880s until the Mexican civil war of 1910-21, European and American conglomerates dominated Mexico's banking, oil, railroad, mining and manufacturing industries—in fact, every facet of the Mexican economy except for agriculture and handicrafts.

These experiences made Mexicans deeply suspicious of all foreigners, especially Americans; and the story of these invasions and domination by foreign powers has been the core of the history taught in their schools ever since.

Still today Mexicans tend to view the United States as a "colossus" whose very size, world political leadership role, aggressive economic ways, and "cultural exports" are a constant threat to their well-being and sovereignty.

On an individual basis, the historical Mexican stereo-type of Americans was that they were aggressive, ill-mannered, uncultured, lacking in family values, immoral, materialistic, always in a hurry, arrogant, condescending and untrustworthy.

Even today, Mexicans regularly accuse American businesspeople who go to Mexico of not having enough respect for their country to try to learn its language or anything about its history and culture; and all too often these accusations are accurate.

This derogatory view of Anglo foreigners, particularly Americans, was generally subsumed in the word *gringo* (GREEN-go), which was more or less the Mexican equivalent of the English word, "greaser," earlier used by Americans in reference to Mexican-Americans and Mexicans, especially those living along the U.S. border.

The first professional commercial attempt to resolve this historical failing on the part of Americans was the American Institute for Foreign Trade (AIFT), established in Glendale, Arizona in 1946 by American Air Force General Barton Kyle

Yount to train young men and women for careers overseas. (The school is now Thunderbird the School of Global Management.

"Thunderbird" is a reference to the World War II air force training field originally located on the site of the school.

Each year after its founding, dozens of Thunderbird graduates who had specialized in the Spanish language and Latin American studies ended up working for U.S. companies in Mexico, and the number has grown over the years. There are now hundreds of TSGM graduates in Mexico, Mexicans as well as Americans, who are a permanent and positive part of the business scene, and the school remains the best source of highly motivated and trained candidates for expatriate business careers in Mexico.*

---

*EDITOR'S NOTE: The author of this book is a 1953 graduate of Thunderbird.

The mutual Mexican/American image has also improved dramatically since the 1980s. The word "greaser" is seldom if ever heard any more, and *gringo* has lost much of its early derogatory connotation. In fact, many Mexicans now use *gringo* in neutral references to Anglo foreigners simply because it is convenient. When used in reference to Anglo girls and women (*gringita* / green-GHEE-tah) it is more likely to be affectionate than disparaging.

Generally speaking, the "ugly" image of Americans in Mexico today is more often applied to young tourists who flock to resorts and beaches to drink, get drunk, and make fools of themselves.

Hospitalidad
Making Friends & Influencing People

One of the most delightful historical legacies of the Mexican people is their tradition of extending *hospitalidad* (hohs-pee-tah-lee-DAD) or "hospitality" to friends and guests. No matter how poor Mexicans may be it is a tradition for them to invite friends and guests into their homes and to feel compelled to offer them some kind of food and drink—and lodging as well if they need it, no matter how cramped their quarters.

A vital part of any new business relationship in Mexico is also eating and drinking together, first in restaurants and lounges, and then as the relationship develops, in private homes. And, of course, foreigners who are hosted by their Mexican business associates or contacts should reciprocate at the first opportunity.

Foreigners should also keep in mind that one of the elements of the hospitality syndrome in Mexican culture is that it compels them to be overly generous with their money, particularly when it comes to paying restaurant and bar bills. Mexican men in general, but especially those who have a strong macho image of themselves, can be very aggressive in paying bills that rightfully should be shared or paid by someone else. (Separate checks are still a rarity in Mexico except among young people who are in school.)

This situation presents something of a dilemma to people who are normally shy about making a public spectacle out of paying such bills. Letting someone show off their machoism is one thing, but taking advantage of them by unfairly letting them pay bills is something else.

People who regularly hold back on paying bills risk being thought of as lacking in social graces and therefore inferior. Or they are seen as people who willingly put themselves under heavy obligation to whoever picks up the tab.

When foreigners are the hosts, or it is their turn to pay the bill, their choices are to be even more aggressive in getting the bill, or to make arrangements in advance with the waiter to slip the bill to them, or to excuse themselves from the table just before the party ends and unobtrusively pay the tab.

The general rule is that whoever extends the invitation to eat or drink, no matter how casually it may be worded or how informal the occasion, is regarded as the host.

Espanol
To Speak or Not to Speak

The character and personality of Mexicans is intimately linked to the Spanish language—and especially to hundreds of key words in the language that delineate both their character and personality (see *NTC's Dictionary of Mexico's Business & Cultural Code Words*, NTC Business Books/McGraw-Hill).

Culturally speaking, Mexicans are as much products of their language as they are of Mexicanized Catholicism, their combined Spanish and Indian spiritual legacies, and all the historical political and economic influences that went into shaping them.

Mexican Spanish influences both the philosophy and psychology of Mexicans and plays a key role in their everyday behavior on every level of their existence. Generally speaking, it is impossible for a foreigner to get inside the skin of Mexicans without having intimate, practical knowledge of the language.

It is possible, however, to achieve an intellectual understanding of Mexican values, beliefs and behavior through study, observation, and intimate contact over an extensive period of time—and to develop an emotional rapport with Mexicans that is personally very satisfying.

Having said that, there is no substitute for being able to speak Spanish well if a person is in Mexico for any purpose and particularly so if it is for business. Although a growing number of Mexican businesspeople in the international area speak good-to fluent English, foreigners who leave communication up to the Mexican side leave themselves open to communication gaps and misunderstandings as well as to being manipulated.

Bilingual foreigners with years of business experience in Mexico advise that visitors who feel their Spanish is adequate to carry on a conversation should start out in that language as a courtesy. They add that if Mexicans speak English fluently and see that the foreigners are in trouble they will normally switch to English as a courtesy on their part ("and sometimes to show off their own language ability," adds a bilingual expatriate businessman).

Stimulating conversation about art, literature, philosophy, politics, sports and national and international events is a national pastime among Mexicans who regard themselves as intellectuals and they take great pride in their skill in expressing themselves verbally. Those with fewer intellectual pretensions are more likely to talk about their families.

All Mexicans, regardless of their economic or social level, are also compulsive users of quotes and humor, especially short jokes. As in the U.S. and elsewhere, a great deal of the humor used by Mexican men is sexually oriented.

Foreign businesspeople in Mexico, including those who do not speak Spanish, are invariably called upon to participate in such conversations (in English), particularly during the very common two-to-three- hour lunch periods.

It goes without saying that on these occasions foreigners should refrain from making derogatory remarks about Mexico that might be out-of-place, upsetting or just bad manners. They should also refrain from knocking their own country. Instead of gaining points with their Mexican associates, such behavior makes them appear small-minded.

Establishing close personal relationships is essential to succeeding in business in Mexico. Adds Key Inter-national's Jack Scott: "The importance of establishing a personal as well as a business relationship cannot be over-emphasized. Many of my customers have spent time in my home in Scottsdale, Arizona and in my cabin near Flagstaff—and I've seen the Grand Canyon so many times I've lost count."

Scott did not stop with inviting his Mexican customers to his home. Each year he sent out 250 copies of the Christmas issue of *Arizona Highways* magazine, along with several yearly subscriptions, to decision makers. He included a personal note with every mailing.

"On my first visit after the New Year I was always greeted with something like 'Thank you for the *Arizona Highways* magazine. My son takes it to school.' Or, 'My wife shows it to all of her friends.' Little things like that set relationships in concrete."

Among other things, Mexican culture makes it virtually mandatory that they ask questions of a personal nature regarding family, schooling, work, and so on, when they are introduced to new people. Part of this compulsion is ordinary curiosity. Another part is an innate need that Mexicans have for quickly determining the character, personality and relative social status of newcomers so they will know how to behave toward them.

The ability to speak Spanish naturally facilitates this process. So no matter how you look at it, not being able to speak Spanish is a disadvantage that should be taken seriously. However, even with the advantage of speaking Spanish well and being familiar with the customs of the country, doing business in Mexico is not a fully satisfying experience for everyone. Comments one foreign businessman who went to Mexico well prepared and lived there for many years:

"My biggest personal disappointment with the Mexican people is that no matter how much effort you make to learn their language and history, and how much you respect their customs, etc., they seem to be unwilling to reciprocate, at least while you are physically in Mexico.

"Perhaps this has to do with the fact that in Mexico there has never been a sense of justice and fairness. The person who is the biggest *cabron* (kah-BROHN), or "son-of-a-bitch," always wins. Also, Mexicans tend to adapt things from Anglo culture that suit them, such as consumer goods, but they are basically resistant to adapting such *gringo* values as punctuality, keeping promises, speaking directly, social activism, and so on. This is very real and can be very frustrating."

Obscenidades y Vulgaridades
Obscenities and Vulgarities

For centuries Mexicans were conditioned to suppress their own individuality and conform to precise forms of behavior that had become institutionalized and sanctified as the only acceptable etiquette. Their lives became one continuous performance in carefully prescribed roles.

Mexicans did not have the option of refusing to play the role that was prescribed for their social status. This resulted in reverse psychology taking over and compelling them to exaggerate their role-playing, whether it was paying respect to someone or cussing them out.

Because virtually all Mexican behavior is, in fact, programmed role-playing, they can be as rude, as insulting and as blasphemous as they can be courteous, all in the blink of an eye. Like master actors, they can switch effortlessly from one character to the other.

Mexican Spanish is especially rich in obscenities, vulgarities, double entendres and slang terms that Mexicans use with demonic relish. There are also hundreds of Spanish words that look very much like English but have slightly or totally different meanings that can cause newcomers fits.*

Huevos (WAY-vohs) can mean eggs or balls (as in male gonads), depending on the intent of the speaker and the verb that precedes its. *Coger* (coh-HAYR) may mean to catch, grab, pick up, or fuck, depending on the context. Said one veteran Spanish-speaking American business expatriate: "It is better *never* to use the word *coger* in Mexico!"

---

*Slang terms and ordinary words with vulgar connotations vary significantly in Latin America, notes Jack Scott. While *huevos* can be a no-no in Mexico, it is okay in Argentina. In Cuba, papaya is slang for scrotum, so you ask for *fruta de bomba* (FRU-tah day BOHM-bah). In Venezuela, *chingona* (cheen-GO-nah) is a dice game played in bars.

Mexicans often say that it is impossible for someone to be a true Mexican until he masters the use of the word *chingar* (cheen-GAHR). There are so many uses of this word that it has its own dictionary, and is probably the only single word in any language to be so honored. ("Although the many meanings of *madre* or "mother" also provide an interesting study"—Ronald C. Walker.)

Chingar is used to mean such things as to hate, to hurt, to destroy, make a fool of, take advantage of, molest, penetrate by force, rape, and so on. It is the key word in a variety of insults, the strongest of which is in combination with the word mother, which results in an especially potent expression.

Mexican men who are good friends use various forms of *chingar* to each other when they are in informal situations. They also use it compulsively when they are angry at someone. But it is not wise for the outsider to engage in any kind of obscenity or vulgarity duel with Mexicans, no matter how fluent one might be. Generally speaking, it is better to avoid even the casual use of such words.

Mexican men (and women!) who regularly attend profess-ional wrestling matches have developed the use of obscenities into a special art form, and are notorious for the skill and vehemence with which they use them. There are few if any people who can best angry Mexicans in the use of foul lan-guage, and it doesn't pay to try.

La Realimentacion
Feedback Mexican Style

There are few things more crucial to manufacturing efficiency and quality control than accurate, timely *realimentacion* (ray-ah-lee-men-tah-cee-OHN) or "feed-back." This presents Mexi-cans with a cultural dichotomy that has traditionally been a serious handicap in the economic development of the country.

Because of the hierarchical, authoritarian nature of Mexican society over a period of many centuries presenting someone with "negative feedback," whether this meant revealing mistakes that had been made, being the carrier of bad news, or criticizing or questioning a plan or project, was considered disrespectful and was generally taboo.

Throughout Mexican history directly questioning or criti-cizing a superior in government or in business, no matter how diplomatic or constructive the action, was something that could have especially serious consequences.

In other words, only positive *realimentacion* was culturally acceptable, resulting in a society in which there were no objectively measured quality control standards for any facet of government or business.

In this environment, both quality control and productivity were more or less personal things that were determined by the experience and idiosyncrasies of the individuals involved. As a result of this situation, about the only high-quality products made in Mexico were those produced one-at-a-time by professional craftsmen.

The use of both negative and positive *realimentacion* in the manufacturing process did not really begin to catch on in Mexico until the appearance of several hundred foreign-owned *maqui ladora* (mah-kee-lah-DOH-rah) plants in the 1960s and 1970s. But since adoption of foreign-style feedback requires a fundamental shift in Mexico's cultural values, the pace of the change has been slow and spotty.

Foreign companies setting up manufacturing operations in Mexico generally must include educational programs to reorient their Mexican managers and employees in the importance of negative as well as positive feedback.

And, of course, these reorientation programs must be carried out in an atmosphere of respect for the sensitivities of all concerned. Mexicans have no trouble at all in understanding the value of feeding back the bad as well as the good. They just have to be convinced that it is safe for them to do so, and then develop experience in the process. "This," says Ronald C. Walker, "is particularly true of constructive criticism, which is such a new element in Mexico society."

Adds Key International's Jack Scott: "For some time to come, *la realimentacion* will continue to be a major challenge in Mexico's developing its industrial base. Scott notes that many of his customers that set up plants to manufacture printed circuit boards (PBCs) in Mexico, including some of the world's largest international firms, eventually closed them down because they were unable to meet the necessary quality control requirements "despite bringing in engineers from the parent companies and training Mexican engineers at the parent plants."

The primary problem was consistency. Said Scott: "The production would be acceptable for a few shipments, then fail to pass the required standards the next time. It was simply that the management and workers could not understand that with electronics 'almost good enough' is not acceptable."

Scott attributed this ongoing problem to lack of motivation. He said that while management and upper-level employees usually had plenty of perks to keep them happy, bench workers and "grunts" had little or none—a situation he said was mostly caused by management providing special "incentives" to the heads of company *sindicatos* (sin-dee-KAH-tohs) or "unions" to soften their demands.

Realidad
Dealing with Mexican Reality

It seems that the less control people have over their daily lives the more they are inclined to create their own fantasy worlds in which they are ostensibly in charge. In such societies, the unreal becomes the real. Or, in more modern terms, virtual reality becomes reality, at least for the people involved.

The pre-Columbian Indian empires of Mexico as well as the Spanish colonial regime (1521-1821) that followed them treated common people more or less like puppets. They were controlled by their race, their class, the Church, the state—even the geography into which they were born and raised. This environment resulted in Mexicans creating a world in which spirit, dignity, pride and passion, expressed in the stylized etiquette and customs that are now generally described as Mexican culture, became the only world they knew.

Personalism, machoism, "project-ism," *manana*-ism, and all the other facets of traditional Mexican behavior were products of this virtual reality.

One of the many facets of Mexican *realidad* (ray-ah-lee-DAD) or "reality" that impacts directly and fundamentally on business is their custom of equating words with actions and deeds, of saying things and then behaving as if they are an accurate representation of reality. In the Mexican context of things, such words represent the ideal world; the way they would like for things to be. But the words do not necessarily reflect reality, or mean a firm commitment that they will do everything possible to make them come true.

Of course, the historic reason for this *realidad* cop-out—for not following through and actually making things happen—was that it was practically impossible. There were simply too many cultural, civil and ecclesiastical barriers.

It was not until the latter part of the 1900s that these barriers began to give way to a more rational, pragmatic view of the world. But it will no doubt be a number of generations before the millennia of conditioning in creating false realities can be exorcised from the national character of Mexicans.

In the meantime, both foreigners and "reality-based" Mexicans alike must continue to deal with this character syndrome in business as well as political affairs. The only practical recourse is an ongoing effort to reprogram the thinking and behavior of the individual concerned, continuous follow-up aimed at keeping everyone and everything in a reality mode, and an incentive factor to encourage willing cooperation. And this, says Dirk Weisheit, is something that is extremely difficult to do.

Fatalismo
Life without Hope

Mexicans, especially those in the lower classes, have traditionally tended to believe that fate was the deciding factor in their lives and to routinely blame unseen, uncontrollable, forces for their lack of success and any bad luck they encountered. This belief was a product of their religious conditioning and the authoritarian governments under which they had lived since ancient times.

Mexico's indigenous Indian religions taught the people that their fate in life was determined by the gods, that they had no say in it. Their social class was fixed at birth. Their lives, including their names, were controlled down to the smallest detail by their sex and place in society.

When the Spanish conquered Mexico in 1519-21, they established a political, religious and economic regime that in some ways was even more limiting and onerous than the earlier

Indian systems. Ordinary people had few if any rights and were generally treated like property by both the state and the Church.

Under the new Spanish regime, the lives of most Mexicans were fixed at birth in a permanent state of poverty. They had no hope that things would change for the better. The Catholic Church programmed them to believe that there was virtue in their suffering and that they should expect nothing more.

The military dictators who ruled Mexico following independence from Spain worked closely with Church leaders to continue denying rights and opportunities to all but a small, elite group of people, perpetuating the *fatalismo* or "fatalism" that had become an integral part of the psychology of the poor.

It was not until the end of Mexico's long and bloody revolutionary war in the early 1920s which basically pitted the poor against the military dictatorship and the Church that the mass of Mexicans began to see the first glimmers of hope for a better future.

There were some genuine improvements in the overall lot of the people over the next 50 years, but only recently has a significant percentage of the masses been able to contemplate an environment of hope rather than despair.

Notwithstanding the enormous progress that has been made in Mexico in recent decades, most Mexicans are still mired in poverty and still have limited opportunities to improve their situation. Their legacy of more than three hundred years of cultural conditioning in servitude and *fatalismo* (fah-tah-LEES-moh) also continues to color their attitudes and behavior.

This fatalistic outlook, which is characteristic of most Mexicans, cannot be wished or legislated away. It will disappear only after the conditions that created it in the first place have long since gone. Until that occurs, one of the most important challenges facing foreigners setting up business operations in Mexico is to establish a management mode that will help employees overcome their fatalistic attitudes by encouraging them to take a more positive and responsible approach to their work.

Abrazo
The Spirit of Mexico

There is, perhaps, no better public manifestation of the emotional, human side of Mexican life than the custom of the *abrazo* (ah-BRAH-zoh), which literally means "embrace."

The *abrazo* originated in the Christian Church in medieval times as part of a ritual ceremony when new priests received their habits and new knights their armor and swords. From there it spread to the Spanish Court, then to the families of nobles and finally into the upper and middle classes.

Spanish *conquistadores* brought the *abrazo* to Mexico in the early 1500s, and it remains today one of the most distinctive features of Mexican culture.

Mexican women embrace each other, but the *abrazo* is primarily seen as a male thing and is still generally associated with middle and upper class men. Friends who have not seen each other for a while—a few months or even a few weeks—first shake hands and then embrace each other, (with the right arm going over the right shoulder and the left arm going under the left arm), firmly patting each other on the back with the right hand two or three times.

If the two friends have been separated for a relatively long time the embrace and back-patting may be followed by another warm hand-shake, often using both hands.

The *abrazo*—practiced only among older friends, not new acquaintances—is indicative of the emotional side of the Mexican character and the close intimacy of their personal relationships. When Mexicans choose to greet foreign friends with an *abrazo* it is an unmistakable sign that they consider the friendship close and important to them.

Because the *abrazo* is a Mexican custom it is not something that should be initiated by non-Mexicans. That could and probably would be taken as presumptuous. But once a new Mexican friend makes the first move, it is appropriate to respond to it enthusiastically.

When Mexican women embrace it is common for them to kiss each other on the cheek—or more often than not, just touch cheeks in a simulated kiss, even in office situations. When

Mexican men embrace female friends it is also common for the men to kiss them lightly on the cheek, or to make the gesture of kissing.

Rancheras
The Heart and Soul of Mexico

Any true understanding and appreciation of the traditional *Mexicanidad* (May-he-cah-nee-DAD) or "Mexican-ness" of Mexicans must include the *rancheras* (rahn-CHAY-rahs) or "country songs" that are a staple of the *mariachi* repertoire. These songs reveal the heart and soul of Mexicans in a way that is not possible for any other medium.

Rancheras are about anger, death, destruction, drinking, fighting, frustration, honor, joy, love, love-lost, pride, sadness, self-pity, weeping—all the things that make up the psyche and national character of Mexicans.

Rancheras are both the life-songs and death-songs of Mexicans. They are the history of Mexicans distilled into words and music, and are played over and over like some eternal refrain that constantly reminds them of the pain of their past.

The emotional content of *rancheras* is so powerful that it engulfs Mexicans in a kind of cultural rapture, exacerbating their feelings to the point that they sometimes think they are going to explode, and must relieve the pressure by drinking, singing, fighting, having sex, or engaging in some other deeply satisfying activity.

Foreigners doing business with Mexicans should keep in mind that the emotional factor in their *Mexicanidad* often takes precedence over practical attitudes and behavior, and must be addressed before any meaningful relationship is likely to develop.

Foreigners who want to participate in the Mexican cultural experience themselves, enjoying it to its fullest and impressing their Mexican friends at the same time, should also be aware that nothing beats learning several of the more popular *rancheras* and being able and willing to belt them out at parties and on other appropriate occasions.

Mexicanidad
The Nature of Mexicanism

Mexicans are fascinated by the nature of their own character, and spend a lot of time analyzing and trying to explain themselves—a trait that is typical of all people whose traditional attitudes and behavior have been molded within authoritarian cultures because such cultures always create fundamental contradictions in their psychology.

As is also typical of such societies, the primary aim of religious and political authorities is to maintain the status quo, which means intellectual creativity that might lead to change cannot be tolerated.

Historically in Mexico's authoritarian non-creative culture, the *way* things were said and done was as important, if not more so, than what one said or did. Form generally took precedence over content, and was used to mask a wide variety of self-abasement, frustration and violence.

Over the generations, Mexicans obsessively questioned and analyzed their existence, their character and their spirit. But because they were not able to change things and were conditioned to look to the past instead of the future, most of their energy and effort went into trying to perfect and sustain an idealized image of themselves—an image that was made up of a combination of Indian spirituality, Catholic theology and Spanish-Arab male chauvinism.

This image was a volatile mixture of pride, dignity, courage, sexuality, and emotionalism, all held together by a highly stylized but tenuous courtesy that depended on absolute conformity by everyone. When this courtesy broke down, the result was invariably an explosion of verbal or physical violence.

Because Mexicans were forced to suppress their natural curiosity and creativity in religious, political and economic matters the reality that they created for themselves was ephemeral; and in the words of philosopher Octavio Paz, was characterized by carelessness, negligence, pomp, passion, and reserve.

Paz adds that Mexico's large number of annual festivals explain the mystery of how Mexicans could put up with the anger, frustrations, pain and sorrow that was so much a part of their history, and still be warmhearted, kind, generous, and bubbling with the joy of life most of the time.

According to Paz, Mexican festivals are not events designed for relaxation and fun; they are great rituals for exorcising the pain and suffering that people endure during normal times—exorcism that is accomplished by getting drunk, shouting, crying, singing, dancing, fighting and sometimes killing.

It was not until the latter part of the 20th century that the religious, political and economic situation in Mexico had evolved to the point that Mexicans could question the validity of the virtual world they lived in, and begin to develop a more rational and practical attitude. But the self-abasement that was so much a part of the lives of ordinary Mexicans over the generations continues to haunt them. The brutality and sadism that is still characteristic of criminals, large numbers of policemen, and the military is attributed to these feelings of inferiority.

The uncommon amount of violence among young Hispanic males in the United States is also said to be a symptom of their feelings of being different, of being inferior, and having to prove their existence and their worth by forcing people to recognize them even though this recognition may be as delinquents and even killers.

Mexicans in general are now making a valiant effort to eradicate these historical demons from their psyche. But the task is formidable and controversial. For one thing, most Mexicans do not want to become "Americanized."

They may not totally like themselves the way they are, but they dislike the negative aspects of Americanism more. When they experience even mild confrontations with Americans the result is usually a surge of aggressive Mexicanism.

The challenge for both Mexicans and Americans is to understand and tolerate their mutually offensive characteristics, and to emphasize those that are positive.

Aviso
Underestimating Mexicans

Many old cultures, particularly in Asia, put a premium on modesty and restraint when people represent themselves to others. Trying to impress others by emphasizing one's educational and work background, much less speak in a boastful manner, is regarded as arrogant and overly aggressive, if not immoral.

Mexico's traditional etiquette, which could be considered more Oriental than Occidental, has almost exactly the same forms and standards of modesty and restraint as China, Japan and elsewhere in Asia when people speak about themselves—and this calls for a clear *aviso* (ah-BEE-soh) or "warning" to foreigners who are not familiar with this cultural syndrome.

Like their Asian cousins, Mexicans have been conditioned for centuries to downplay their intelligence and talents, and when in the presence of superiors and those with authority, to behave in an obsequious manner.

Unfortunately, Americans and other Westerners who are inexperienced in such cultures typically assume that such behavior is at best indicative of a passive, submissive personality, and at worst indicates either a low order of intelligence or a genuine lack of ability—or both.

Because of this syndrome, many Western business-people, usually those who do not speak Spanish and are not familiar with Mexican history, tend to treat their newly met Mexican counterparts with a condescending attitude that is perfectly obvious to everyone—a response that reveals more about their own cultural myopia than anything else.

Just as obviously, this kind of behavior will not win friends or influence people. (In fact, as in the case of China and Japan, history shows that when this kind of condescending behavior is carried to an extreme it can have devastating political, military and economic con-sequences.)

A growing number of Mexican businesspeople are as well educated, as experienced, and as sophisticated as any of their foreign counterparts, and underestimating them is both unwise and dangerous. The challenge is for both sides to keep in mind is that in cross-cultural affairs everyone generally benefits from the merging of positive values and processes rather than attempting to impose one on the other.

(4)
THE MEXICAN
WAY OF DOING BUSINESS

Mastering Cultural Administration

A key to understanding the "Mexican way" of doing business is to recognize that business management in Mexico has traditionally been an application of cultural attitudes and customs, not the objective, pragmatic function that is associated with management in the United States and other practical-minded countries.

Unlike Americans and others, Mexicans have never viewed work and their private lives as separate entities. They therefore did not develop a separate set of principles and guidelines for each area. Rather than attempting to conduct business on the basis of mathematical formulas (still favored by some American business schools), Mexicans have traditionally taken a personal and therefore arbitrary approach to business.

The first and foremost factor in any business consideration in Mexico is almost always cultural, and must be approached from that viewpoint. This means that skill in human relations exercised within the appropriate cultural context has traditionally been the primary qualification for success in business.

While the formulaic approach to management favored by Americans is making inroads in Mexico, the cultural mode continues to prevail. Foreigners wanting to succeed in business in Mexico will therefore find that a Master of Cultural Administration, or "MCA," will get them further than an MBA.

Adds Key International's Jack Scott: "Generally speaking, Mexican businessmen will tolerate 'cultural indiscretions' only when it is in their favor to do so, such as when they have a real need for the product or service being offered."

Confianza
The Importance of Trust

In the United States and other Anglo countries business relationships are generally based on accepted practices and laws
that describe and limit the obligations of each party. In this
environment, cultural practices are important in setting the style
and tone of the business relation-ship, but laws pertaining to the
situation take precedence over everything else. The legal obligations of each party is seldom if ever out of mind.

Traditionally, this was not the way business was done in
Mexico. There were a variety of laws during the 300-year
Spanish regime and the following 100 years of home-grown
dictatorial rule, but these laws either did not detail the process
of business or protect the interests of the parties involved, or
they were not enforced because of rampant corruption.

For more than 400 years Mexicans could not go into business within a framework of laws that could be depended upon to
either guide them or protect them. Generally speaking, the only
protection they had were the personal bonds they had established with the various entities concerned. Their existence and
any success they achieved were based on personal *confianza*
(cohn-fee-AHN-zah) or "trust," not on laws.

Still today business in Mexico is based more on the trust that
exists between the parties concerned than on laws. There is now
a substantial body of laws designed to control business activities, to protect consumers, and redress wrongs, but as in the
past the justice system is often incapable of enforcing these
laws.

Probably the greatest challenge facing foreigners wanting to
do business in Mexico is becoming acquainted with the "right"
people and then developing the mutual trust that is necessary
before any project can get off the ground.

Added an expatriate businessman: "You can get anything
you want in Mexico. You just have to find the right person to
get it for you. If you hit a roadblock, look for someone else to
help you. Depending on the situation, you may want to start at

the top. However, if you bypass the lower-level people and they are the ones who have to make the decision, you're screwed. This is often the case when dealing with bureaucrats who do the grunt work, and can delay your papers if you don't 'follow the rules.'"

The process of developing *confianza* is not something that can be done with one or two meetings. Depending on the size of the project and the risk involved it can take months to years, and involve dozens of meetings and an extraordinary emotional investment.

While prices and the quality of products and services are important in Mexico—and increasingly so as the economy develops—the most important ingredients in the first stages of doing business in Mexico are the personality, character and manners of the foreign individuals involved. If these personal qualities are not on a sufficiently high level to impress and satisfy the Mexican side, the relationship is not likely to go anywhere, regardless of how technically competent the foreign side might be.

On those occasions when deals are made without the normally required personal foundation, for whatever reason, they usually fall apart within the first two or three years because the bonds are not strong enough for the two sides to accommodate each other in times of stress.

Foreign businesspeople should keep in mind that when they encounter a problem in Mexico, regardless of its nature, the best way—and sometimes the only way—to resolve it quickly and completely is with the help of Mexican friends in high places who trust and like them.

Palancas
The Leverage Syndrome

As is invariably the case in hierarchical, authoritarian societies, it is generally *who* you know and how obligated they are to you rather than what you know or what your technical skills are that leads to success.

Mexico is no longer a purely vertical society and its government and professional institutions are no longer totally authoritarian. But for the most part, having personal contacts in the right places, with the right amount of power, is still the way that things get done efficiently.

Still today a great deal of the time and energy of Mexicans, especially those in business and politics, is spent creating and nurturing personal contacts that they can call on for support or help of some kind, whether it is to get a business license, a contract, or solve some strictly social problem.

This method of doing business is often described in terms of using *palancas* (pah-LAHN-cahs) or "levers" to achieve goals. In some cases, absolutely nothing can be achieved without a *palanca*. In virtually all situations, if "leverage" is not applied things will move forward very slowly. Generally, the larger the new enterprise, the more leverage is necessary to move it forward.

In the past, the people with the most powerful leverage were almost always politicians because they con-trolled the authority to do business and how it was done. Politicians are still vitally important in the business process in Mexico but their power is no longer absolute.

A new breed of politician actually seeks opportunities to help businessmen, and business executives of large and important companies have assumed some of the leverage once monopolized by government officials.

Foreign businesspeople planning on doing business with Mexico are generally well-advised to make identifying and nurturing the appropriate *palancas* a key part of their advance preparations. The most efficient way for newcomers to Mexico to accomplish this important first step is to retain the services of a consultant who has the necessary qualifications: is bilingual, bicultural, has years of online experience in Mexico, and is well-respected in the Mexican business community.

El Patron
Bossism in the Board Room

In Hispanic cultures, loyalty between employees and employers has traditionally been based on personal relationships; not on abstract principles. This led to the development and glorification of the *patron* (pah-TRON) culture in which owner-bosses ruled with absolute authority over their employees, did not delegate authority, did not accept criticism, and demanded total loyalty.

Mexico's still existing *patron* system is also related to the *cacique* (cah-CEE-keh) or "chief" system that was traditional in Indian tribes and nations. Generally, the position of *cacique* was hereditary and was imbued with all of the respect and power that comes from having been sanctified by generations of time.

Present-day *patrones* (pah-TROH-nays) in Mexico, particularly those in rural areas, towns, and smaller cities throughout the country, still enjoy most if not all of the authority, respect and loyalty that has traditionally been given to their predecessors.

The term *patron* itself is more or less neutral. Bosses who are in legitimate businesses as well as leaders of criminal gangs are customarily addressed as *patron* with-out any negative overtones in either case.

Foreigners should keep in mind that *patron* is a personal title that is generally used only by inferiors addressing superiors within an established relationship. An outsider or stranger would more likely address people in charge by their professional title or the universal *Señor* So & So.

Adds an expatriate American businessman: "Another title of special importance in Mexico is *licenciado* (lee-cen-cee-AH-doh), which is almost always used when addressing government bureaucrats.

A number of business categories in Mexico, from agriculture to construction, are dominated by *patrones*, with the result that their presence and way of operating impacts on foreigners doing business in those areas. Basically, it means that foreign companies in these categories must adapt to dealing with single, powerful individuals, rather than working with groups of managers and building consensus from the bottom up.

In some cases, the *patron* system can be very positive because individual bosses do not have to confer with anyone else. They can make fast decisions and order things done as they see fit.

Part of the power of the *patron* system comes from its paternalistic nature. Bosses generally look after their employees more or less as if they were their wards or children, playing a role in their personal affairs as well as their work. Expatriate businesspeople in Mexico who have employees are naturally expected to think and behave like *patrones* to some degree. This includes exhibiting a personal interest in the lives of employees outside of the office or factory.

Generally speaking, the more personal the relationship between employer and employees, the more loyal and diligent the employees will be. One facet of this personal relationship is simply to know the names of employees, recognize them each day by greeting them, and occasionally stopping to talk to them.

Added veteran Mexican hand Jack Scott: "When the foreign businessperson is walking through the plant of a customer or supplier in Mexico and can greet foremen and workers by name, ask them about their new baby or some other personal matter, the results can be very positive.

"If the workers are using equipment sold by the foreign visitor they will take better care of it and have more pride in using it. The power of the bench worker and shop foreman should not be underestimated when it comes to recommending new or additional equipment to management."

La Mordida
Paying the Price

Another aspect of surviving and doing business in Mexico that outsiders must learn to deal with is the age-old institution of *la mordida* (lah mohr-DEE-dah) or "the bite." In plain words, *la mordida* refers to all of the bribes, "fees" or "commissions" that individuals and companies have to pay to people directly and sometimes indirectly involved in the matter at hand.

Mordida ranges from small payoffs to street cops to avoid getting tickets for some real or imagined offense, and smoothing the way at Customs and Immigration checkpoints, to huge sums of money paid to high-level politicians and others to buy their support or their silence.

The Mexican government, particularly in recent years, has made a concerted effort to at least reduce the incidence of *la mordida*, with some success. Higher level business deals in present-day Mexico can sometimes get through without any special fees or commissions.

But *la mordida* has been an institutionalized part of the Mexican culture for so many centuries—and the underlying reasons for it have not yet been addressed— that it will surely be two or three generations before it is significantly diminished.

The origin of *la mordida* no doubt goes back to ancient times when subjects would present gifts to kings, chieftains, priests and others in power to keep them friendly. The need to stay on the good side of those in power was imperative because there were no laws protecting common people from them.

This situation became even worse during the Spanish colonial period in Mexico (1521-1821) because the salaries of officials and bureaucrats were deliberately kept low—often far below the subsistence level, virtually forcing them to "charge" for their services.

By the last decades of the colonial period, Mexico's government as well as the Church (which owned more than half of all the real estate in Mexico and had a larger income than the government) was almost totally corrupt from top to bottom, and *la mordida* had become so deeply embedded in the political and economic systems that there was no way to separate them.

Following Mexico's independence from Spain in 1821 *la mordida* continued to plague both Mexicans and foreigners visiting and doing business in the country. It was not until the reform-minded Carlos Salinas became president of Mexico in 1988 that a serious effort began to eliminate some of the most conspicuous abuses of *la mordida*, particularly at border immigration centers.

This effort had only minimal success, but it was enough to get the cleanup process started and to make sure that it would stay on the agenda of future political leaders.

It is now rare for high-level government officials to demand, expect or accept bribes. They are more likely to consider the offer of a bribe insulting, especially if the offer is made by a foreigner. A realistic-minded businessman added that if you want to offer a bribe or must offer one to someone it is better to have a Mexican do it for you.

Businesspeople approaching Mexico with fairly sizeable projects can sometimes avoid most "bites" by announcing up front that they have no budget for paying any kind of special "fees" and that they are depending on their would-be Mexican partners to help them get through unbitten.

On a lower, more personal level, as when face-to-face with someone who is threatening to cause a lot of delay, trouble and expense, the best advice from those with experience is to pay up and mark it off to the cost of doing business. ("How to do this is best left up to accountants"—Dirk Weisheit.)

Of course, giving in to the system not only helps to perpetuate it but can also cause all kinds of problems for foreign businesspeople and their firms because *mordida* is, in fact, illegal.

Michael T. Eakins elaborates: "I strongly disagree with anyone who advises that on many occasions the best solution involving hints or demands for *la mordida* is to pay up and bear it. In the first place, it is illegal and can get a person and his/her company into serious trouble. In the second place, by paying bribes, especially to government officials and company executives, you are not only supporting but condoning an evil that is responsible for preserving the unacceptable status quo.

"It is important to keep in mind that once you give in to the pressure to pay you will have to continue paying, often in larger and larger amounts as the 'biters' take advantage of your compromised position. If it becomes obvious that a project is probably not going to happen unless someone is paid off, the best solution is to distance yourself from the situation and turn the problem over to your Mexican counterparts."

The only known antidote for *la mordida* is *amistad* (ah-me-STAHD) or "friendship." Mexican businesspeople spend a lot of time making and nurturing friendships with key people in banks and in local and national government offices both to expedite getting things done and to avoid having to pay for the services.

Knowing the right person in a Customs office, for example, can save one anywhere from hundreds to thousands of dollars on one shipment of goods. Of course, such friendships involve obligations that must be repaid in some way to keep the *amistad* ledger balanced. These repayments may be money, in kind, or tit-for-tat favors.

Newcomers who are not familiar with the nuances of fulfilling such obligations—so that they have a positive rather than a negative effect—should consult with a local veteran. Knowing how to repay an obligation is as important as knowing what kind and how much payment to make.

Adds Jack Scott: "In all of the years that I worked in Mexico, I never paid *mordida*. I anticipated the problem and took steps to avoid it. I found that friendship worked better than a bribe, and that the individual did not lose face. As an example, I discovered that the plant manager in a certain company who recommended equipment purchases had a chronic dental problem and was unable to get a toothpaste that would eliminate the condition. I consulted with my own dentist who recommended a special medicinal brand.

"On my next trip to Mexico I took a dozen tubes of the paste, gave them to the plant manager and told him my dentist had suggested that he try it. The treatment worked. For years thereafter when I visited that plant manager toothpaste was part of my luggage. Over the same years he was instrumental in his company buying over $4 million worth of equipment and supplies from my company.

"Not *mordida!* Just helping a friend."

Scott continued: "The purchasing manager of a major multi-national company, one of my best customers, heard that I was planning a visit and called to ask a favor. He wanted me to bring him a 'matrimonial size' mattress. I told him it would be difficult for me to get a double-bed size mattress on a plane as part of my luggage.

"He replied that it would not be a problem. Finally, after a prolonged discussion, I discovered he was referring to an inflatable mattress that he wanted to use for camping. I took him the mattress. He insisted on paying for it, so I finally quoted him a price that was one-third of what I had paid. Not *mordida* but *amistad!*

"I also made a practice of bringing toys for customers' children and gifts for secretaries. When I packed these things in my luggage I always put them on top so they would immediately be seen by the customs officers. I explained to the customs officers why I was bringing them to Mexico and added that if they had children of their own they could take a toy or novelty for them.

"This sometimes depleted my stock of toys and gifts, but I was never asked about the hundreds of dollars worth of carbide drills I might be bringing in for a customer with an emergency. Developing *genuine* friendship at all levels pays greater dividends than cash."

Despite the growing number of foreigners who are able to maneuver their way around paying *la mordida* the custom continues to flourish. It especially remains difficult, and is often impossible, for Mexicans to avoid paying up.

Newspaper surveys confirm that people in every class and category in Mexico, from housewives to street vendors, are involved in soliciting and/or paying bribes. Two common occasions that can be especially costly: getting a home hooked up to public water, and avoiding a fire inspection of a business.

La competencia
Competition Mexican Style

Competition in the Darwinian sense of survival of the fittest provides much of the energy that fuels the American way of life, from childhood play, sports and mating, to politics and the economy. Darwin would have missed his calling in Mexico. Generally speaking, Mexicans are not culturally programmed to compete with each other, and regard both personal and group competition as disrupting to the point of being immoral.

Rather than having been conditioned to compete against each other for everything, Mexicans have traditionally been programmed to sublimate their personal desires and think in terms of their families and cooperative groups.

The Mexican attitude toward competition extends to management and union relations as well. Mexican unions generally work in close cooperation with management, and view the adversarial relationship that typically exists between American unions and American corporations as totally irrational.

At the same time, says a veteran expatriate business-man, foreign managers in Mexico can always expect their unions to fight, although their actions may be symbolic. Foreign corporations that attempt to introduce a competitive culture into their operations in Mexico without extensive reorientation in advance invariably meet all kinds of passive resistance from their Mexican employees. Those that have been the most successful in doing this have used trained Mexican employees as the primary instructors.

Personal competition, particularly the blatant cut-throat kind that is common in larger American corporations, is especially offensive to Mexicans. They compete with each other but it is generally done in a soft, subtle way that is designed to avoid direct confrontations.

Foreign companies operating in Mexico must take this cultural view of competition into consideration in virtually everything they do, from their management style to how they interact with other companies in the same industry.

American style competition is gradually making in-roads into Mexico, especially among the *maquiladora* factories along the U.S.-Mexican border and the large multinationals. But over-all its effect is still minimal and foreign companies from competitive societies must adjust their approach if they want to succeed.

Negociaciones
Mexican Style Negotiations

Generally speaking, Mexicans do not view negotiations as an inclusive process that is supposed to result in iron-clad agreements or contracts that bind both sides to precise actions and obligations.

To Mexicans the end result of business negotiations—an agreement or a contract—is just the first step in relationships that will evolve with time, changing as the circumstances change, and are therefore something that should be approached slowly and carefully.

Like the Chinese, Japanese and other Asians, Mexicans engageed in negotiating business agreements characteristically give precedence to personal and human factors rather than to the "business" details involved in the situation. Such things as time-frames, prices and profits often appear to be secondary.

Also like their Asian cousins, Mexican negotiators are masters at using the "good guy, bad guy" technique, and in putting negotiations on a purely emotional level (by emphasizing how poor Mexico is and how much they need help, etc.) in order to gain as much advantage as possible.

Not surprisingly, Mexicans are just as susceptible to emotional appeals as Americans and others, if not more so, and foreigners who learn how to be less logical and more emotional generally make out better in Mexico than anyone else.

Mexicans negotiators also get great mileage out of their famed courtesy, personal warmth and effusive hospitality. When combined, they can virtually disarm their foreign "opponents." In fact, this kind of cultural seduction is one of the biggest challenges facing foreign businesspeople in Mexico.

Because Mexicans see written contracts as little more than formal symbols of the intent to become partners, the important thing to them is the character of the individuals involved, how trustworthy, how dependable they are.

The many meetings that Mexicans usually require before they are ready to negotiate the terms of a contract are primarily aimed at judging the character and personality of the people involved, and finding out if the culture of the foreign company is compatible with the business culture of Mexico and the realities of the Mexican marketplace.

Prior to scheduling negotiating sessions, Mexicans want to know precisely who is going to be present from the foreign side —names, titles and specialties—and details of the agenda...all information that should be provided to them in writing. It also pays to have the key points of the presentation written in English and Spanish.

The foreign side should request the same information from their Mexican counterparts, making a point that they know who the senior member of the Mexican team is and who will be presenting the contract to the president or chairman for signature.

Junior members of Mexican negotiating teams usually arrive early to make sure all of the arrangements are in order. Senior members may be accompanied by an entourage that includes interpreters (and bodyguards).

In keeping with the personal and social nature of business in Mexico, negotiating sessions normally begin with several minutes of casual conversation. Any attempt to start the proceedings quickly may be perceived as rude.

Mexicans negotiators generally do not respond in precise, concrete terms that make their feelings and intentions perfectly clear. They prefer to speak in somewhat ambiguous and esoteric terms that leave their position open to various interpretations. Another factor that hinders communication in Mexico is that Mexicans involved in negotiations or other kinds of business dialogue will typically indicate they understand something when they actually do not—the reason being they do not want to embarrass themselves or to upset the speaker.

Mexicans consider it impolite to say "no" or to flatly turn anyone down. They are more likely say something like, "maybe," "we'll see," or "let's discuss it later." And generally, it is not too much of an exaggeration to say that in Mexico one should never take "yes" as a final affirmative answer.

Thus one of the key challenges facing foreign negotiators in Mexico is to gradually and diplomatically narrow the different readings they get from their Mexican counterparts. Some obvious pointers:

1) Be well-prepared and know who you are talking to.
2) Keep a united front.
3) Use lots of visual aids.
4) Do not put all of your cards on the table up front.
5) Never lose your temper.
6) Never make threats.
7) Don't be upset by relatively long periods of silence from the Mexican side. Periods of silence are an important part of the Mexican [and Asian] negotiating techniques.
8) Don't try to fill every silent period with talk. Relax, rest, review your notes, or hold quiet side conferences with your team.
9) Don't be pushy or show signs of impatience but make it clear that there are time constraints that you must follow.
10) Emphasize the economic and social benefits to Mexico.
11) Apologize before and after for any possible cultural transgressions.
12) Do not bring lawyers to the first meeting unless pre-arranged.

Naturally, the larger and more important the project, the more imperative it is that communication be absolutely clear and accurate. This brings up two key points that often cause foreign companies problems without them being aware of it.

First, there are some potentially very serious disadvantages to sending Mexican-American employees to Mexican. If they have not been educated in Mexico, had extensive business experience there or received special training in the U.S., they usually do not speak contemporary Mexican Spanish fluently and are especially weak in technical and professional business vocabulary.

As one Anglo expatriate points out: "Mexicans expect Anglos to make errors in Spanish, but when Mexican-Americans make mistakes they lose credibility. Besides, some Mexicans do not like Mexican-Americans no matter how good their Spanish might be, and make no effort to disguise their feelings."

Second, Mexican interpreters hired for the occasion by outside firms are in a very awkward position that often detracts substantially from their ability to represent the foreign side impartially and accurately. They are Mexicans first and interpreters second, and except in rare cases cannot separate themselves from that fact.

Just as important, the Mexican side expects interpreters in this category to be on *their* side because they are Mexican, putting a special burden on the interpreters and disadvantaging the foreign companies using them.

Some obvious approaches to eliminating or reducing these problems: Foreign companies employing Mexican-Americans to deal with Mexico should make sure they have had or receive the special training that is necessary to bring their language ability up to par; and foreign companies should not depend only on Mexican interpreters hired by the other side when they are involved in crucial negotiations.

In using interpreters in general it is vital that they be thoroughly briefed prior to meetings. It is just as important that those using interpreters speak in simple, measured words, and in short paragraphs.

Even when there has been no indication that any member of a Mexican negotiating team understands or speaks English, foreigners should assume that someone on the team does, and not make any side remarks to interpreters, or anyone else, that they do not want the Mexican side to overhear.

Because of the importance of personal relationships in doing business in Mexico foreigners have a tendency to leave legal matters to the last in their negotiations, thinking they will be easier to handle that way. Veterans scarred by experience say it is better to bring all legal issues up at the beginning of negotiations. One added: "You can bring up legal issues, but let their lawyers tell you what to expect. They are the experts."

Another vital point that may be a bit surprising in view of the Mexican tendency to be very laid-back in doing business: Mexico's legal requirements are very formal and very strict. Every document that is to be registered or filed must be precisely as prescribed by law, which means it must be an original, with every "i" dotted and every "t" crossed.

Once an agreement has been reached and a contract signed there is typically a let-down in the pace of activity on the Mexican side so it is important to have consistent, diplomatic follow-up to help keep things moving for-ward.

Leaving things up to lower or middle Mexican managers can be especially disappointing because there are numerous cultural taboos that prevent them from taking the initiative. They generally act only when they receive direct, specific orders from above. Trying to motivate lower managers directly or indirectly by appealing to their personal ambitious, as Americans especially are wont to do, is therefore usually meaningless.

Generally, the only effective approach is to inspire the top person in the company. Adds Michael T. Eakins: "When negotiating in Mexico, especially with junior executives when their superiors are present, it is very important to always leave room in your final proposal for slight reductions in your price or a slight easing of your terms so that your Mexican counterparts can gain 'face' in front of their colleagues by demonstrating their ability to 'win' the game.

"Failure to do so can seriously damage a relationship that probably cost you a great deal of time and money to develop because the people you have been dealing with will lose face in front of their bosses."

Outsiders should also keep in mind that getting through negotiating sessions is often the first and most crucial test of their ability to do business in Mexico.

Inspeccion y Calidad
The Supervision Phobia

The personalism, dignity and overwhelming need for respect that are part of the traditional character of Mexicans may be impressive in social settings, but these same traits can be, and often are, serious barriers to the conduct of business.

Historically, Mexicans were conditioned to take everything personally, making it difficult or impossible for them to react to things objectively. This meant that corporate executives, managers and employees, as well as government officials, generally took any kind of criticism of their work as a personal affront, no matter how obviously constructive or diplomatic the criticism might be.

They tended to regard any kind of criticism as demeaning their dignity, and therefore calling for some kind of reprisal rather than self-reflection on their part or any positive change in their attitudes or behavior.

Criticism as well as close *inspeccion* (in-speck-SHE-ohn) or "supervision," including instructions on how to perform any kind of task, have also traditionally been regarded by Mexicans as an assault on their self-respect. Their attitude was that criticism and precise instructions on how to do things was a blatant sign that they were not trusted, and was therefore disrespectful.

Mexican employees expected to be told exactly *what* they were supposed to do, and generally waited for orders from their superiors. Typically when they were not given precise tasks to accomplish they remained idle, or did personal things.

The other side of these cultural beliefs was that superiors, particularly those on higher executive levels, felt it was beneath their dignity to spell out to subordinates *how* they should do things, or to closely monitor and control their activities. This, of course, resulted in a Catch-22 situation in which there was very little sharing of experience or knowledge, and limited co-ordination.

The more hierarchical the management, the less genuine communication there was between the various vertical levels of administration, and therefore the less control management had over productivity, quality and customer service.

These cultural obstacles combined to make it virtually impossible for companies to maintain high levels of quality control or to predict when deliveries could be made, and so on. In a very broad sense, executives, managers and workers were all in a world of their own, doing their thing their way, with little or no input from the outside and apparently no concern for what others were doing.

Although these cultural attitudes and practices are still very much alive in Mexico, it is now generally recognized by executives of larger enterprises—and smaller firms with international experience—that these factors are incompatible with a competitive economy, and efforts are being made to replace them with objective thinking and self-motivated behavior.

The challenge presented by these deeply entrenched cultural beliefs and customs is enormous, however, and it will no doubt be a generation or more before they can be significantly changed on a national basis.

At this time, companies that have succeeded in rationalizing their corporate philosophies and management systems are still in the minority.

Foreigners going into partnerships with Mexican companies must therefore evaluate the cultural profile of the executives and workers of each firm on an individual basis, and be prepared to create educational and reorientation programs as they are needed.

One cultural problem that most foreign managers of new expatriate enterprises in Mexico must contend with is problem-solving. Veteran expatriate businesspeople in Mexico repeatedly emphasize that their Mexican counterparts are great at planning but not at problem-solving because it involves questioning, criticizing and changing things, all of which have traditionally been taboo.

Attempts to solve problems must therefore be handled with considerable skill in order to avoid damaging egos and creating emotional backlash.

Embutes
Manipulating the Press

Given the personal nature of both business and politics in Mexico it is not surprising that most of the news media has historically reflected the same morality and engaged in the same kind of personally oriented practices as politicians and businesspeople.

A significant aspect of the relationships between individual journalists and the business and political establishment was summed up in the word *embute* (emm-BOO-tay), which figuratively translates as "pay-off."

Mexican businessmen and politicians have traditionally paid off journalists (and editors) to make sure that they suppressed information that might impact negatively on them, and published only "news" that would benefit them.

It has also been common for some Mexican news-papers to manipulate the public by printing extra large, boldfaced headlines about some spectacular event or scandal, with no related article or story anywhere in the paper.

Since the buying of the press was institutionalized by the government itself, it quickly became entrenched in the overall political and economic systems of the country.

Over the decades many journalists became well-to-do, and sometimes quite wealthy, as a result of investments and side-businesses financed by the *embutes* they received.

In 1994 the Ernest Zedillo administration began a serious attempt to curtail the *embute* practice by exposing corruption within its own ranks. This political move encouraged the publishers and editors of a number of the country's leading daily newspapers to mend their own ways, and there are growing signs that these efforts have been successful to some degree.

By 1995 several major newspapers were routinely reporting on the crimes of people on the highest political and business levels—an obvious sign that neither their editors nor any of their writers were being paid off.

There is no possibility that such exposes will totally eliminate the *embute* practice, however. That would require the reformation of the whole ethical system.

Foreign businesspeople should continue to be very cautious about getting caught up in the *embute* trap. The wisest procedure is to announce (repeatedly) that corporate policy makes showing "favoritism" of any kind to the press totally taboo, and put that policy on a personal basis by adding that if you should break the taboo it would mean your job.

La Cultura
Culture Comes First

Mexican society is still tightly organized in a vertical structure. Authority and power are generally centered in individuals rather than offices or titles. There is often more than one "chain of command" in a company, and one of the challenges is finding out who really has the power on the different levels of management.

In both business and politics in Mexico real power is generally in the hands of *influyentes* (in-flu-YEN-tehs) or "influential ones." These are people whose connections, reputations, intellect, deeds, charisma and so on—often combined with whatever degree of ruthlessness is necessary to get things done—are the so-called movers and shakers in their communities.

Another cultural factor of vital importance is that it is still not routine for executives in Mexico to share information with their subordinates because knowledge has traditionally been regarded as part of their appurtenance of power and is used to demonstrate that power.

As a result of this custom, lower management and employees in general are often working more or less in the dark, and are not in a position to make decisions even if they have the authority to do so.

Mexican executives are famous for getting excited about the prospect of undertaking new projects, and for their ability to plan new enterprises. But their hang-ups about sharing information, delegating authority, monitoring the activities of middle managers and employees, and demanding timely results, often negates their initial enthusiasm and good intentions.

Foreigners dealing with Mexican companies must, of course, take these cultural factors into account. One way of doing so without causing top management to lose face is to emphasize that the project at hand is a team effort which requires that everybody involved be fully informed and responsible, and then follow through to make sure that happens.

Here too, about the only practical approach to this problem—pioneered by several foreign companies—is to first re-program managers in the concept of dividing the work force into teams, giving each team the information and authority its members need to do their job, then letting them know they are responsible for seeing that the work is done well and on time.

Generally speaking, it does not do any good to make a complaint or request to an ordinary employee or to a low-ranking manager in a Mexican company because they have no power to act and are not likely to pass either one on to a senior manager. About the only recourse is to go directly to the top or as high as possible in the management hierarchy, keeping in mind that this approach may back-fire if someone down below has any say-so in the matter.

When a problem occurs on the factory floor of a foreign operation in Mexico the most effective procedure is to go directly to the senior manager without bringing it up to the worker involved. This way the worker does not lose face and the senior manager gains face by taking care of the problem. However, it is especially damaging to verbally *threaten* to go over someone's head.

Mexicans invariably view problems of whatever nature from a personal and emotional standpoint, making confrontations virtually inevitable. Generally the best way to avoid confrontations or defuse those that develop is to use experienced third parties as intermediaries.

The relatively slower pace of business in Mexico generally also extends to paying debts. Customers often have to be repeatedly reminded by personal calls to pay up. "They will always promise, but will not always pay!"—Dirk Weisheit.

There can be many reasons for slow payment other than a poor cash position. Poor management in the accounting department, lack of organization, or something personal like favorites of the accounting clerks being paid first, are also common.

In such situations, about the only solution (where larger companies are concerned) is to apply *amistad* indirectly, says Jack Scott. He explains: "Paymasters are usually in a remote location and are never seen. I have always depended upon the plant managers who need an uninterrupted supply of my parts and products to act as my 'agents.' Each month I sent the plant managers a fax listing the invoices that were over thirty days past due. If they were good friends, the fax was usually sufficient to get prompt payment. Among other things, the plant managers wanted to demonstrate that they could get things done."

In addition to their national pride and highly charged self-image, Mexicans tend to be especially sensitive to any patronizing manner by foreigners. Americans are more apt than most to commit this cultural error because their historical image of Mexicans has generally been negative and a condescending attitude has been built into the psyche of many people.

Etica Laboral
The Mexican Work-Ethic

Mexico's *etica laboral* (eh-TEE-cah lah-boh-RAHL) or "work-ethic" has typically been described by anthropologists, historians and others as "working to live" as opposed to the "living to work" attitude that is usually associated with Americans and others raised in the traditions of work being a religious obligation.

But this old image of Mexicans was, and still is today, misleading. For one thing, it stemmed in part from the extraordinary number of fiestas staged each year in Mexico. Another factor was that there has traditionally been a small but very conspicuous class of Mexicans who did not have to work for a living, and chose not to.

Other even more important factors include the fact that large numbers of Mexicans, especially those living in towns and cities, could not find jobs in the first place, and over the generations large numbers also suffered from poor nutrition and various kinds of debilitating stomach ailments that made vigorous activity impossible.

Historians say that Mexico's "work to live" *etica*, especially among the elite, can be traced back to the nearly 800 years during which the Moors occupied Spain (711-1502). They say that during this long period virtually all manual labor in Spain was done by the Moors and by Jews, while Spanish men, particular those in the middle and upper classes, eschewed manual labor altogether, devoting themselves to the arts and to warring against the Moors.

Following the expulsion of the Jews in 1492 and the Moors in 1502, the refusal of Spanish men to work with their hands became so serious that it threatened the economy of the country. Spain avoided national bankruptcy only because of the gold and silver that began pouring in from Mexico and its other Latin American colonies in the mid-1500s.

Even with this wealth from the new world, the problem of middle and upper class men not wanting to engage in any kind of productive activity continued to plague Spain for generation after generation, with the government growing more desperate.

Among the various steps the government took in an effort to get Spanish men to work was a decree issued by King Carlos III (1716-1788) affirming that work was an honorable activity no matter what class one belonged to. (Historians add that the decree was ignored.)

In any event, the Spanish conquistadors who conquered Mexico in 1519-21, and the Spanish administrators and fortune hunters who followed them brought this deeply entrenched aversion to manual labor with them.

During the subsequent 300-year Spanish regime in Mexico virtually all labor in the country was done by Indians and the new race of disenfranchised Spanish-Indian Mestizos who, by 1810, outnumbered the Spanish administrators and the Mexican-born Spaniards combined.

This tradition was continued following Mexico's successful rebellion against Spain in 1810-1821, and it was not until the mid-1900s that a genuine middle class made up of Mestizos who were not adverse to working with their hands began to emerge.

Still today most upper class Mexicans and many in the middle class regard manual labor as beneath them. It is taken for granted that lower class people are hired as drivers, gardeners, maids, etc.

But this is not to imply that Mexicans in general do not work hard when they have the opportunity or when they need to. Among the poor in both urban and rural areas, working 10 to 12 hours a day every day is often a matter of survival. The professional class generally works from 10 to 12 hours a day if you include their two and three-hour lunches.

But at the same time, lower class Mexicans learned long ago how to live relatively full and meaningful lives in what the Japanese call "clean poverty," meaning having enough food not to go hungry and enough other material things to ensure minimum comfort but nothing extra or special.

One Mexican who had spent more than 10 years as a farm laborer in the U.S., working 10 to 12 hours a day, often seven days a week, summed up one aspect of the Mexican work ethic very succinctly.

"Why in hell should we work hard here in Mexico when it doesn't pay? Here you don't get paid for working hard! You can't get a job because you work harder than the other fellow! In Mexico it isn't what you are but who you are that is important!"

In the meantime, American style materialism is replacing Mexico's traditional culture of clean poverty—something that Mexicans are very much aware of and resent to some extent because they see it as also eroding all the other cultural values that they regard as superior and prefer to keep.

Historically, Mexico's human values were different from those in the U.S. and other Anglo societies. While American and other Anglo businesspeople generally gave preference to technical competence and other production-related and sales-related activities, Mexicans emphasized "people skills."

In the majority of Mexican companies individuals who are most likely to go up through the ranks to high managerial and executive positions are those who are the most skilled at human relations; who are good at "reading" people, attracting their support and loyalty, and making a good impression on both company people and outsiders.

This reason accounts in part for the fact that many high-level personnel in Mexican companies are not familiar with the details of their companies' operations. Another reason is that managers and executives often owe their positions to family connections rather than their own skills or accomplishments.

However, with the advance of computer-controlled machinery and high-tech manufacturing in general, this is changing. In newer industries, it is usually engineers who are on the fast track. At the same time, managers in all areas are expected to get results, and there are some very tough, very aggressive Mexican managers.

One of the great challenges facing the majority of Mexicans today is how to raise their standard of living to a satisfactory level without sacrificing their traditional living-comes-before-work ethic.

More and more middle and upper class Mexicans, especially those involved in international business, are getting around this dilemma by adopting the philosophy followed by the legendary entrepreneur Mario ("Mike") De La Fuente of Nogales, Sonora, whose life-time motto was "I work like a Gringo and play like a Mexican!"

Nepotismo
Family Members First

Nepotism is alive and flourishing in Mexico for two very simple reasons. Throughout the history of the country people were not protected by laws and could not depend upon any institution or anyone except family members and close friends.

This circumstance gave rise to an exclusive family system, including godmothers and godfathers, and dependence upon networks of family members and friends, as well as the *patron* system in which individuals give their loyalty to a boss in exchange for him protecting them and guaranteeing their welfare.

The other reason for the high incidence of *nepotismo* (nay-poh-TEES-moh) or "nepotism" in Mexico is the fact that from the beginning of the Spanish colonial period in 1521 well over half of all industry in the country was dominated by a small number of families who received huge land grants from the Spanish Crown. These grants included all of the Indians and industry within their areas.

During the dictatorial reign of Porifiro Diaz from 1877 to 1910 several American family clans (the Guggenheims, Rockefellers, Morgans, Hearsts, etc.) were among those who dominated virtually all industry in Mexico other than handicrafts and farming.

Still today well over half of the wealth and industrial power of Mexico is in the hands of a few hundred families which naturally continue the family traditions of nepotism. One often hears or reads of "the one thousand families" in reference to the concentration of wealth and power in Mexican.

More often than not when foreign companies begin looking into the possibility of doing business in Mexico, in whatever industry or region, they find that the leading players are family groups. Just as often, the same families have a lock on local politics.

Any change in this situation will be an evolutionary one that takes place over a number of generations, and will not mean that the dominant families will disappear. It means only that they will be joined by other families that have succeeded in building their own empires.

The power yielded by these families can be a great asset for foreign companies looking for partnerships, but if they are going to compete with these family monopolies they better have deep pockets.

Some foreign corporations operating factories in Mexico have found that making use of the traditional nepotism in finding new, trustworthy employees is, in fact, an advantage. Employees gladly take some responsibility for family members or relatives who are hired by their company. These companies take the position that there is nothing innately wrong with such a policy as long as the individuals concerned are capable of doing the jobs they hold.

One American businessman with long experience in Mexico related the work-place discrimination inherent in nepotism to the degree of personal information that is included in job resumes and application forms, and requested by interviewers. The questions routinely include such things as parents' occupation, parents' and spouse's income, and religious affiliation.

Nepotism among the professions and in government is another matter, however. It remains one of the most corrupting influences in Mexican society, impacting on all the domestic and international affairs of the country by precluding competition, often preventing the best from rising to the top and encouraging personalism instead of professionalism.

However, *nepotismo* in government is more susceptible to change than nepotism in business, and it may be that Mexico will eventually have a government that is at least partially operated on a merit system.

Notes Michael T. Eakins: "Ernesto Zedillo, elected to the presidency in 1994, was one of the first contemporary Mexican presidents who did not come from a rich, powerful family. He was a poor boy from Sonora who worked his way up through the system."

In the meantime, foreigners dealing with Mexico must contend with the personalism that is bred in both business and government by the deeply entrenched custom of *nepotismo*.

Regatear
Bargaining as a Social Exercise

Foreigners not experienced at bargaining in public markets or across negotiating tables are often at a serious disadvantage in Mexico, where the practice is regarded as an important social skill and is something of a national pastime.

Mexicans look upon the give-and-take of bargaining as a social exchange that takes some of the exploitation out of business activity by personalizing and humanizing it, and they enjoy it as other people enjoy games.

In sharp contrast to this, many people, particularly Americans and other Anglos, are inclined to regard bargaining with a jaundiced eye, essentially viewing it as an irrational and ultimately devious way of doing business.

This contrasting view of bargaining is especially conspicuous in tourist-oriented curio and gift shops along the U.S.-Mexican border. Shopkeepers expect their customers to bargain, and set their prices accordingly. When customers do not bargain and pay the full asking price, the attitude of the proprietors is that they are naive or dumb...or so arrogant that they will not stoop to bargaining and therefore deserve to be over-charged.

Visitors shopping in Mexico should enter into the spirit of the custom. If they maintain a pleasant, friendly manner and make reasonable counter offers—10 to 20 percent off of low-priced goods and 20 to 30 percent off of higher priced items—they can almost always walk away with a bargain.

In business negotiations in Mexico the foreign side should reserve some margin or benefit that it can use to "sweeten the pot" in exchange for something from the Mexican side—a process that satisfies the bargaining urge.

Abogados y Chicanas
Lawyers and Delaying Tactics

Mexico's judicial system is based on the Napoleonic Code, which means, among other things, that suspects are generally treated as if they are guilty until they prove their innocence. And there is no such thing as trial by jury. Judges decide on the guilt or innocence of people brought to trial.

This system makes justice far more personal and far more dependent upon the political climate. Until 1995 the only qualifications for being a judge in Mexico was that one be an attorney and at least 35 years old. More stringent qualifications for judges were enacted into law that year but it will no doubt be years if not decades before there is any discernible effect.

Mexico's courts are also often so over-loaded that judges render decisions on several dozen cases a day, making the system even more susceptible to abuse. Because of these factors, it is very important for companies or individuals in Mexico who are accused of some crime to be represented by capable attorneys.

There are many good *abogados* (ah-boh-GAH-dohs) or lawyers in Mexico. There are also many who are less than capable because the judicial system requires only that they have a bachelor's degree in jurisprudence. They do not have to pass a bar examination (there are none), and no review board of any kind measures the qualifications of lawyers or monitors their behavior.

Another factor in the legal system in Mexico that can have a far-reaching and costly impact on doing business there is the institutionalized use of *chicanas* (chee-CAH-nahs) or "delaying tactics" by lawyers for the defense.

A lawyer can delay a trial for up to six months simply by filing a protest that the opposing attorney is not qualified to act as counsel on that particular case.

Lawyers can use other *chicanas* to drag cases on for years with few if any sanctions by the court. One of these tactics is simply to ignore the orders of the court to present a case. It is the custom that lawyers can ignore such orders four times before they are sanctioned by the court, and the fourth time the penalty is only a nominal fine.

Decisions handed down by judges are often not the end of things because lower courts do not have the authority to enforce them. One of the results of this situation is that most decisions are automatically appealed to successively higher courts.

Money, not justice, is the "oil" of the legal system in Mexico. In fact, it was the legal system in Mexico that sustained the universal practice of *la mordida* or "the bite" from the beginning of the country's colonial period under Spain in 1521.

Judges themselves are generally not for sale outright, but the process that surrounds and supports the legal system, from copying to filing documents, requires payoffs, usually in the form of *gratificicaciones* (grah-tee-fee-cah-cee-OH-nehs) or "tips," every step of the way.

Having the advice and direct help of a capable and well-connected *abogado* is therefore crucial to getting in and staying in business in Mexico.

Foreign businesspeople should keep in mind, how-ever, that Mexicans do not like to deal with attorneys in the early stages of negotiating any kind of a new arrangement. They prefer that attorneys not be brought in until the two parties have reached an agreement and the only thing left is to finalize the details of the contract.

A package of reforms designed to eliminate much of the personal element and introduce fairness and actual justice into Mexico's judicial system was decreed by President Ernesto Zedillo in January 1995. Prior to the decree, there were 26 justices on Mexico's Supreme Court. All were appointed directly by the president, for life. They, in turn, appointed all lower court judges.

Zedillo's decree was aimed at exorcising this incestuous situation. The new law required all justices then on the Court to retire, reduced the number of Supreme Court justices to 11, changed their tenure from life to 15 years, and made it mandatory that appointees appear before the Senate in open hearings, and receive a minimum vote of two-thirds of the Senate in order to be confirmed. But this new legislation does not guarantee fairness.

The judicial reform law also created a selection committee consisting of representatives from the three branches of government to appoint judges and magistrates to the two lower levels of the federal court system. These reforms—the first since the 16th century, according to one Mexican critic—were loudly applauded by Mexico's business community but it was understood that significantly positive effects would be a long time in coming.

It will, no doubt, be decades before the reforms filter down into the system and result in significant changes in the judicial culture of the country because they must occur in concert with other economic, political and social changes.

As a final bit of "legal" advice, one expatriate businessman says: "Foreign businesspeople in Mexico should never even think about suing!"

La Comida
Power-Lunching in Mexico

For businesspeople in Mexico the lunch period, and increasingly the breakfast period as well, are often the most important times of the day. For Mexicans, lunch—not supper or dinner as in the U.S. and most other Anglo-European countries—has traditionally been the main meal of the day, as well as an important social event.

Rather than being a short noon-time break to allow people to eat a quick meal and go back to work, the traditional Mexican afternoon meal was a major break in the work-day during which people did such things as take care of personal affairs, nap (because they were normally up late), met with friends for two or three hours of stimulating conversation, or engaged in romantic rendezvous.

Lunch in Spanish is *almuerzo* (ahl-MWEHR-zoh), a word that can be misleading since it may refer to a late breakfast or a light snack around noon before the heavy afternoon meal, which is generally referred to as *la comida* (lah coh-ME-dah), meaning the main meal of the day.

The evening meal is called *merienda* (may-ree-EN-dah) if it is light and *cena* (SAY-nah) or "supper" if it is heavy. A light snack may be eaten fairly early in the evening, but a heavy meal is usually eaten around 9 p.m. or later.

In contemporary times, the long, leisurely mid-after-noon "lunch" period has become of vital importance to businesspeople in Mexico because it is when they create and nurture the personal relationships that are the foundation of their business ethics and activities.

Another development that dates from the 1980s are breakfasts meetings, which interestingly enough, seem to be preferred by a new breed of government officials who are apparently anxious to get as much as possible out of their workdays.

Mexican businesspeople do conduct meetings with outsiders in their offices. But these are formal or semi-formal occasions that are generally short and perfunctory. Or they are formal negotiating sessions after the two sides have gotten to know each other by participating in a number of Mexican style lunches.

Some consultants on doing business in Mexico say that foreigners who do not learn how to "do lunch" Mexican style cannot do business in the country and may as well not waste their time trying. This is not a total exaggeration, for it is during these long lunch periods that Mexicans take the measure of their foreign visitors, judging them on their personality and character, on their educational level and cultural sensitivity, and decide on whether or not they want to do business with them.

Lunch time in Mexico generally begins at 1 p.m. and lasts until 3 (in some places the hours may be 2 p.m. to 4 p.m.). There are occasions, however, such as when there is something to celebrate or when drawn-out discussions are taking place that "lunches" last until 5 or 6 p.m.

Foreign businesspeople visiting or resident in Mexico are well advised to acquaint themselves with two or three of the best restaurants in the area, and make themselves known to the owners, managers and head waiters so they will be recognized and welcomed when they bring their Mexican associates there.

Drinking alcoholic beverages, usually beer or wine, is common at *la comida*, and is part of the tradition of dispensing with formal etiquette, getting a little tipsy and letting the cares of the world go by. Foreigners hosting such affairs should offer their guests drinks, and follow the lead of their Mexican guests (but pace themselves).

Hosting a lunch or supper in Mexico is very much like it is in the U.S. and elsewhere. Whoever extends the invitation is expected to pay the bill.

Foreigners should keep in mind, however, that Mexicans are normally very aggressive in their efforts to pay restaurant and bar tabs because that is part of their image. They will often go to extremes to pay bills, even when they can't afford it.

The best way to avoid getting into a tug-of-war over restaurant and bar bills is to inform the waiter in advance who is to get the bill, or excuse oneself from the table a few minutes early and pay the bill before the party breaks up.

Foreign businesswomen in particular must take the initiative in paying restaurant bills when they host Mexican businessmen. The more macho the men the more honor-bound they feel to demonstrate their mastery by treating the women as their guests. Key International's Jack Scott adds:

"The foreign businessperson should not under any circumstances initiate a business discussion during *la comida*. If a business subject is brought up by the Mexican businessperson the response should be low-key and appropriate to the occasion.

"One should not expect to conclude business deals at lunch, but rather work on establishing mutual respect and understanding that will make subsequent negotiations a friendly experience. Inviting the plant manager, purchasing manager or service engineer to *la comida* is a high compliment and can pay long-term dividends. It is not common, however, for middle management to participate in *la comida*."

Hablar por Señas
Sending the Right "Body" Message

Mexicans are great users of body language and are especially sensitive to its use by others. Family members and friends are conditioned to have close, frequent physical contact with each other, standing and sitting close, touching, shaking hands and hugging.

When Mexicans friends are standing and talking, the preferred distance between them is about half of what Americans are programmed for. Really intimate friends may stand even closer. This situation makes some Americans and others uncomfortable. But if they move back to a more comfortable distance, they may be subconsciously perceived by Mexicans as cool and unfriendly.

The degree of physical closeness in Mexico is determined by the closeness of the relationship. Strangers keep their distance, psychologically as well as physically, coming closer together only after they have been introduced and begin developing a friendship.

Outsiders should be cautious about trying to speed up the getting acquainted process by getting too close too soon. This can send the wrong message. Best idea is to follow the lead of the new Mexican acquaintances.

Eye-contact is also a key part of the non-verbal language of Mexico. Prolonged eye-contact is an important part of the relationship between equals, but not between inferiors and superiors. Such behavior by an inferior would be taken as insubordination and a challenge.

Thus foreigners who do not maintain good eye-contact with their Mexican counterparts of equal rank, or with someone of inferior status, are sending a message that they are weak, unsure of themselves, and possibly untrustworthy.

Prolonged eye-contact that is not accompanied by a pleasant, friendly facial expression also sends a negative signal that is likely to be interpreted as a challenge. Street-toughs along the U.S.-Mexican border are said to take even fleeting eye-contact as a challenge calling for a vicious response.

Mexicans commonly use a number of hand signals, includeing raising the right hand chest-high, with the fingers together and the back of the hand facing outward, as a way of saying "thank you." The "thumbs up" sign is fine, but older and old-fashioned Mexicans may regard the familiar American sign for OK—the index finger touching the thumb to form a circle—as an obscene gesture.

Clinching a fist and thrusting it toward someone is a common way of obviously expressing anger. When Mexicans point at someone they use two fingers or the whole hand. The index finger is generally used only when accusing or berating someone.

Holding a hand up and "writing in the air" is commonly used in restaurants to signal "bring the bill."

Men who stand around or walk with their hands in their pockets are considered low-class and uncultured—an impression that obviously can have a negative effect on their potential as business partners.

Again as in the Orient, when you want someone like a waiter or clerk to come to you a common hand gesture is to hold your hand out, palm down, and wave it up and down (as if you were signaling goodbye in other cultures). This gesture should be used only to clerks or other service personnel, or to children or close friends.

El Vestido
Dressing for the Occasion

Mexicans are exceptionally sensitive to wearing apparel because for centuries what people wore was a conspicuous sign of their social and economic status. Each class of people in the country wore styles of clothing that were associated with their race and social standing. Craftsmen, workmen and others also generally wore apparel that identified their trade.

In this cultural setting it was very important for people that they did not "dress down" and be taken for a lower class than what they really were. The higher their social class, the more pretentious their favored apparel.

In present-day Mexico, the racial-social implications of apparel are not as overwhelming as they were during the 300-year Spanish period or the 100 years of dictatorial rule that followed. But how one dresses continues to say a lot. Middle and upper class Mexicans still tend to be quite formal in their dress, and they still equate apparel with social rank, education, and success.

Businessmen in particular are judged by what they wear. Armani suits are very popular among both the business and political elite.

Foreign businesspeople should not ignore the importance of image in Mexico, and should dress up to enhance their own. Mexicans assume automatically that an expensively dressed person is a successful person, and is therefore someone worth knowing and possibly doing business with.

"Successful people or people in general who want to be taken as successful keep their shoes shined and wear cologne and jewelry, especially gold chains and Rolex watches," says Dirk Weisheit.

However, in smaller cities, towns and rural areas there is definitely such a thing as over-dressing. Wearing conspicuously expensive suits, shoes and accessories in these settings is likely to be resented by local businessmen and government officials because of the image they have of "city slickers" from Mexico City and other major metropolitan areas coming in to take advantage of them—an image based on actual experience over many generations.

The *guayabera* (y-yah-BAY-rah) shirt, adds Dirk Weisheit, is virtually de rigueur in Merida and Yucatan. In provincial cities that are hot and humid during the summer months, such as Culiacan, Hermosillo, and Mexicali, or tropical all year around (like La Paz), business dress is usually slacks and shirts. And, advises Michael Eakins, when setting up meetings in such places it is perfectly acceptable to ask your Mexican counterparts to advise you on the appropriate dress.

Until the 1980s about the only Mexican women who wore slacks or pants suits were *putas* (PUU-tahs) or "prostitutes," a factor that often put slacks-and-pants-wearing foreign female tourists in awkward positions.

The influence of imported TV shows and movies, coupled with more affluent Mexican women traveling abroad, has resulted in a conspicuous change in this attitude. However, veteran expatriate businesspeople in Mexico, both men and women, advise that foreign women doing business or attending social functions in Mexico should avoid "aggressive" attire.

Buena Presentacion
Making a Good Impression

Making a good impression in Mexico naturally goes well beyond wearing apparel, and is subsumed in the phrase *buena presentacion* (BWAY-nah pray-sen-tah-CEE-own), which literally means "good presentation."

By *buena presentacion*, Mexicans mean what people wear, how well they are groomed [from their haircut and hair style to their fingernails], their facial expression, their manner of speaking, the language they use, and what they say.

Mexicans are especially sensitive to both appearance and manner, and equate a *buena presentacion* with a good family background, education and cultural refinement—all things that are associated with social class.

Mexican companies seeking employees for positions that require them to meet the public generally regard *buena presentacion* as the most important qualification.

Foreigners visiting and working in Mexico are judged by the same standard. Outsiders should also keep in mind that in Mexico there is a big difference between casual dress and sloppy dress. To Mexicans, people who dress in sloppy clothing or behave in a sloppy manner have no pride, no class.

Regalar
Gift-giving Mexican Style

Mexican culture differs radically from that of China, Japan, Korea and elsewhere in Asia is in the practice of *regular* (ray-guh-LAHR) or "gift-giving." While giving gifts on a massive scale is an institutionalized part of business, politics and personal relationships in Asia, it plays a relatively minor role in Mexico.

In Asia gifts are given as part of the process of initiating relationships, and thereafter are given to the same people on a regular basis to help sustain the relationships. In Mexico, on the other hand, gifts are generally given only after relationships have been established, and there is no ironclad rule that the gesture be repeated on a regular basis thereafter in order to maintain the relation-ships.

Whether or not gift-giving continues after relationships have been established is more of an individual, personal decision than a cultural imperative. In any event, in Mexico it is better to err by under-giving than by over-giving because Mexicans are very sensitive to such obvious attempts by outsiders to ingratiate themselves.

Generally speaking, the same gift-giving rationale and customs that prevail in the United States, Canada, etc. are also appropriate for Mexico.

An often repeated warning about giving a gift to the wife of a Mexican business associate because it might be regarded as a sexual overture is out-of-date in most of Mexico.

In deciding on what to give a new contact or business associate, one approach is to find out from a third party what his or her special interests are and try to match those interests. Otherwise, just using common sense should be enough. Books, magazine subscriptions, gift certificates, desk accessories, new electronic devices, etc., are almost always safe and satisfactory.

People invited to private homes for afternoon or evening meals usually take liquor, wine or candies. If the foreign visitor chooses to take wine it is best to take an imported brand. Mexicans generally do not think much of domestic wines. Chocolates are especially popular [the chocolate industry was invented in Mexico]. Items for the home or kitchen are also appropriate and appreciated.

Mexican women appreciate gifts of flowers as much as anyone, but there are some cultural factors to be aware of. Red roses, for example, are usually given to sweethearts, while white roses are a sign of mourning. A potted plant is also a safe choice. Gifts that are representative of the giver's home state or home country are especially well-received. In any event, gifts should be modest so as not to put the host under heavy obligation to reciprocate in kind.

Just as people who are invited to meals or parties at private homes generally take gifts of some kind, Mexican hosts who invite people to their homes or elsewhere for special events may give each person who attends a parting gift known as a *remojo* (ray-MOH-hoh).

Remojos apparently serve several purposes: as a demonstration of the hosts' appreciation to those attending the party; as a reciprocal action for those who brought gifts; and as a custom in keeping with the culturally programmed hospitality that is so important to Mexicans.

In a more private sphere, the ancient Indian custom of giving personal things, accessories, clothing and the like, to people who admire them still occurs in Mexico among those whose spiritual outlook is primarily Indian.

Outsiders should therefore be cautious about overly admiring the personal possessions of Mexicans least they feel obligated to hand them over. Attempting to pay can make the situation even worse because that makes it appear like a commercial transaction rather than a sincere gesture of goodwill and sharing.

Tarjetas de Visita
Name Card Protocol

Name cards or *tarjetas de visitas* (tahr-HAY-tahs day bee-SEE-tahs) are especially important in Mexico because of the hierarchical nature of the society. They serve a dual role of identifying company and professional affiliations as well as helping to establish the social status of individuals which determines the appropriate etiquette to be followed.

Many middle and upper class Mexicans have both business name cards and personal name cards. The latter, which give their home addresses and telephone numbers, are used for social purposes.

Exchanging business cards in Mexico, as in Japan and other Asian countries, is generally more formal than in the United States, and there is an etiquette that should be followed if you want to make the best possible impression.

First of all, Mexicans expect business cards to be treated with considerable respect. They should be carried in a card case and kept in mint condition. Giving someone a dirty or worn card goes beyond being rude to them. It also reflects on the character of the person handing out the card.

Name cards should not be "tossed" across a table or passed out in a casual or sloppy manner. After shaking hands, they should be somewhat ceremoniously presented, with the right hand, with the "top" of the card up so that the recipient can read the card without having to turn it over or around. It is also considered rude to put a card you have received in your pocket or in a card case without looking at it and reading it.

If you are seated at a meeting table (or sit down shortly after introductions), you should put the name cards you have received in front of you on the table, preferably in the order in which your Mexican counterparts are seated so you can more readily identify them by name and title during the meeting.

Of course, foreign businesspeople who are resident in Mexico or have local contact addresses and are visiting there, should have their name cards printed in Spanish on one side and in their native language on the other side. Mexicans appreciate it when visiting business people have bilingual name cards.

Writing on someone's business card as a memory aid while still in their presence is also generally regarded a negative. (I sometimes do it afterwards.)

SUMMARY COMMENTS

SUMMARIZING his comments on the challenges of doing business in Mexico, Dirk Weisheit said: "I have found that trusted Mexican friends will freely share tips on how to get along with Mexicans, explain why things are the way they are, and suggest ways of getting around the various obstacles.

"I therefore recommend that newcomers make a concerted effort to establish close friendships with Mexicans, not business associates, who are fluent in English, whom they can confide in, ask questions of, and run ideas by."

Weisheit adds two final notes of caution: "To be successful in Mexico, business approaches should be for the long-term. At the same time, contingency plans should always be in place, no matter how good things appear at the moment.

"Gringos should also avoid getting involved in political discussions, and stick to business. You have to be Mexican to really understand Mexican politics! And Foreigners in Mexico should also avoid street demonstrations of whatever kind."

Another commentator emphasized the point that it does not pay for foreign businesspeople in Mexico to try to "Mexicanize" themselves. He explained: "In the first place, Mexicans don't expect it, and in the second place, any such attempt is likely to be amateurish, make the person appear foolish, and more likely than not turn people off rather than impress them."

The same commentator added that American business-people in Mexico should not be ashamed of being Americans and go around apologizing and putting on a humble act. "Behaving in an arrogant manner will get you nowhere, but humility that is out of place can be just as destructive to a relationship. And if Mexicans wrongfully put the United States down they should be corrected."

He also cautions about belittling Mexico and Mexicans. "Mexicans are very proud. They often point out things that give them pride but that Americans and others take for granted or that do not measure up to what exists in the U.S. and elsewhere. On such occasions, foreigners should bite their tongues."

BUSINESS HOLIDAYS

There are seven annual national holidays in Mexico (for which employees are paid):

January 1 - New Year's Day -Constitution Day - February 5
March 21 - Benito Juarez's Birthday
May 1 - Labor Day
September 16 - Independence Day
November 20 - Revolution Day
December 1 - In presidential election and installation years, inauguration Day, December 1, is also a national holiday.
December 25 - Christmas Day

There are also a number of "secondary" holidays, religious as well as secular, during which businesses close and people take off from work…on some occasions, for several days. These holidays include:

January 6 - Day of the Three Kings
February 24 - Flag Day
April 9-16 - Holy Week (Good Friday and Easter)
May 5 - Cinco de Mayo (anniversary of the Battle of Puebla against the French)
May 10 - Mothers' Day -
October 12 - Columbus Day or "Day of the Race"

November 1-2 - All Saints' and All Souls' Days
December 12 - Feast of Our Lady of Guadalupe

It has also been tradition for a great many Mexicans to observe *El dia de San Lunes* or "St. Monday's Day," by arbitrarily staying away from work on Mondays…a custom that is still fairly common, particularly in less industrialized areas.

Another old custom that persists to the point that it is a problem for some employers is the habit of taking off from work any time one feels like it—a practice that is known as *dias feriados de ganas*, which can be translated as "days taken off because (the employee) wants to."

When holidays fall on Tuesdays and Thursdays it is also fairly common for people to stretch them into four-day holidays by taking off on Mondays and Fridays, a custom that is known as *puentes* or "bridging."

A great deal of Mexico simply closes down during Holy Week. People flock to resorts, especially the more popular beach areas, by the hundreds of thousands, making it essential to get reservations at the more desirable hotels months in advance.

TITLES

Board of directors / *Consejo de administracion*
(Kohn-SEH-ho deh ahd-meen-eess-trah-ssee-YOHN)

Also: *La junta directiva* or *mesa directiva*
(Lah hoon-tah dee-rehk-TEE-bah / may-sah dee-rehk-TEE-bah)

Chairman / *Chairman*

Deputy chairman / *El presidente delegado*
(Ehl preh-see-DEHN-teh deh-leh-GAH-doh)

President / *Presidente* (Preh-see-DEHN-teh)

Vice president / *Vice presidente* (Veess-preh-see-DEHN-teh)

Director / *Director* (Dee-rrehk-TOHRR)

Director General* / *Director General*
(Dee-rrehk-TOHRR Hay-nay-RAHL)

*The chief executive officer (CEO) of a Mexican company is commonly called *Director General.*

Deputy director / *Subdirector* (Ssoob-dee-rrehk-TOHRR)

Company secretary / *Secretario* / (Sseh-kreh-TAH-rree-yoh)

General manager / *El gerente general* (Ehl heh-REHN-teh heh-neh-RAHL)

Manager / *Gerente* / (Heh-RREHN-teh)

Deputy manager / *El asistente al gerentem* (Ehlll ah-sees-TEHN-teh ahl heh-REHN-teh)

Assistant manager / *Subgerente* (Ssoob-heh-RREHN-teh)

Supervisor / *Supervisora* / (Ssoo-pehr-vee-SSOH-rah)

Marketing director / *Director de mercadotecnia*
(Dee-rrehk-TOHRR deh mehrr-kah-doh-TEHK-nee-yah)

Sales manager / *Jefe de ventas* (HEH-feh deh VEHN-tahss

Accountant / *Contador* (Kohn-tah-DOHR)

Attorney *Abogado* / (Ah-boh-GAH-doh)

Corporation / *Sociedad Anonima (S.A.) or Compania*
Soh-see-eh-DAD Ah-NO-nee-mah / Cohm-PAH-nyah))

Corporation With Variable Capital
Sociedad anonima de capital variable (S.A. de C.V.)
(Soh-see-eh-DAD Ah-NO-nee-mah deh kah-pee-tahl bah-ree-
ah-bleh)

Joint Venture *Asociacion en participacion*
(Ah-soh-see-ah-see-OHN ehn Pahrr-tee-pah-see-OHN)

Nonprofit Corporation / *Asociacion Civil (A.C.)*
(Ah-soh-see-ah-see-OHN See-beel)

Noncommercial Corporation (Civil Society) / *Sociedad Civil
(S.C.)* (Soh-see-eh-DAD See-beel)

SELECTED BIBLIOGRAPHY

Condon, John C. *Good Neighbors—Communicating With the
Mexicans*. Yarmouth, Maine: interculture press, inc.

De Mente, Boyé Lafayette. *Romantic Mexico.* Phoenix, AZ:
Phoenix Books/Publishers.

De Mente, Boyé Lafayette. *NTC's Dictionary of Mexico's
Business and Cultural Code Words.* NTC Business Books
(McGraw-Hill).

De Mente, Boyé Lafayette. *There's a Word for It in Mexico.*
New York. McGraw-Hill.

Fuentes, Carlos. *Where the Air is Clear*. New York: The
Noonday Press (a division of Farrar, Straus and Giroux).

Kras, Eva S. *Management in Two Cultures*. Yarmouth, Maine:
interculture press, inc.

*Mexico Business—The Portable Encyclopedia for Doing
Business in Mexico.* Editor: Edward G. Hinkelman. World
Trade Press, San Rafael, Calif.

Moran, Robert T.; Abbott, Jeffery. *NAFTA--Managing the Cultural Differences*. Houston, Texas: Gulf Publishing Company.

Paz, Octavio. *The Labyrinth of Solitude and the Other Mexico*. New York: Grove Weidenfeld.